Friends of Szymon
Foundation

"We are each of us angels with only one wing,
and we can only fly, by embracing one another. "

Rainbow Humming Bird on the Butt
Original title: "Tęczowy Koliber na Tyłku"
Author: Szymon Niemiec
Translator: Jagoda Sochon
Illustrator: Lujeran
Publisher: LGBT Press EU
Copyrights: LGBT Press EU © 2006
ISBN: 978-83-924191-0-5
Pages: 229

RAINBOW

HUMMING BIRD

ON THE BUTT

Life and Art as Seen by Szymon Niemiec

For all the people for whom I live...

Szymon Niemiec
December 2006

FORWARD

This project took two years to complete from the concept in summer of 2006 to the first publication in Polish last summer – which sold out - the English translation took time and motivation. We believe that there could be no better time than now for the release as the world embraces for a change driven by universal hope.

As an American national I personally am hopeful of the kindred spirit between neighbors and nations that is emerging.

Those individuals who have been repeatedly knocked down or ignored within society may soon be empowered and possess the courage to stand-up and fight once more. They cannot do it without exemplary leaders committed to the common good.

The homosexual lifestyle isn't easy but neither is life itself. Each of us has a story no of ours is lesser than any others. It is those who tell the best story who win in the end. The truth always triumphs but sometimes it requires advancement.

A fierce urgency propelled us to release the English version of this autobiography.

The events include our advocacy of criminal litigation against Polish Equality Foundations officers particularly Robert Biedroń & Tomasz Bączkowski. This book sets the record straight and immortalizes others legacies who were at the forefront in establishing Polish LGBT rights.

To give our readers a little background, as we were preparing the book and researching for the court case against the "suspects" Robert Biedroń & Tomasz Baczkowski locating documents and interviewing attorneys, something happened that upset Szymon thus us also. Szymon is a kind hearted guy that helps anyone that needs it. He did not want to write this book in fact nor go to court – I advocated the book and the court proceedings. I insisted and have committed resources to aide in immortalizing his story and exposing those who have not only betrayed him but the goodwill of the international community.

Recently Robert Biedroń a self-anointed "gay activist" made an arrogant statement to the press about Szymon religious beliefs and went further to insist that Szymon had been excommunicated from the Polish gay community. That was the final straw for me.

Why? Because nobody has the authority to excommunicate or exile another human being from society - nobody.

I insisted that Szymon contact his religious and ask them to write open letters if not in his defense in the defense of religious freedoms – no I am not a believer at least not of organized religion. A nice letter from Bishop Diane Fisher's (Metropolitan Community Church) on of Szymons contacts was presented. Several months later her egregious behavior caused me to accelerate the release of this title also. At this point I must explain my own exasperation with the bishop; the author of this title is a strong believer of faith, make of that what you will. He'd discussed and shared with me e-mails between himself and the "bishop" during our work on this book. Szymon was optimistic and believed good fruits would be borne from this relationship. I cautioned him not to be optimistic of establishing a relationship with her or MCC stateside because although this bishop was allegedly responsible for Eastern European dioceses – it meant nothing, at least not to gays in Poland. As you will gather from reading this book Szymon has a tendency, a weakness, of accepting persons at face values. It is his nature as he is not sophisticated to the ways of the "west."

He and the bishop tossed around the ideal of establishing a MCC in Poland which considering the country is 96% Roman Catholic would have been an extraordinary achievement. I was suspect of the "bishop" because there were too many lapses in their communications and I doubted her sincerity. In fairness I as a former US Security and military officer do not accept anyone on face value. My belief is to trust but verify everything and everyone.

Diane Bishop wrote another letter endorsing Robert Biedroń activities in Poland very aware that he is under criminal investigation and of his manipulative and deceitful relationship with Szymon. She did this without reading official documents, contacting sources etc. It is my personal belief that as an alleged spiritual leader this constitutes betrayal and hypocrisy in the highest form.

Her actions underscored my own understanding of how very little the "west" knows about Polish gays and the turmoil which they face establishing a vibrant community. In fact it has been my observation during the research that I have conduct that some of the gay activist use similar Soviet era tactics of fear and intimidation as their former Russian master and political conservative right wing nuts.

The stories which Szymon shares in this writing are typical of the mentalities that permeate the Polish LGBT community.

It truly saddens me that "silence" is the weapon which these scoundrels depend and use effectively similar to the old communist days. Silence is engrained in their history as often oppressed peoples.

My intelligent western colleagues and peers disappoint too for their apparent lack of understanding and motivation to assist worthy activist instead settling on the bull du jour to with superficial qualities, deceptive personas and whorish self-promotion. (I have a book of study of gay culture in Poland to be released in 2009, watch for it.)

Ultimately good and bad fortune does not discriminate from the deserving or undeserving. It is up to those of us who truly care about preserving and protecting that basic human rights for future LGBT generations to answer the call. If we do not we have already failed as a community.

- publisher

Everything started one warm day of July in 2006. I was sitting in my Warsaw apartment with my new American friend LeeAndrew and we were talking about everything that two male adults who've passed through many trials in life, can talk about when they don't have anything else to do.

I was trying to explain to him why I am who I am. I started with a lengthy history. I told him about a few events of my life, which influenced me in making certain decisions. And as it was to appear later, these decisions changed not only me and my life, but also influenced the history of Poland. LeeAndrew was listening to me, asking questions and I saw he was vividly interested in what I was telling him. One moment he told me a story about a Cuban activist for LGBT rights, who wrote his story having gone through great personal difficulties, trauma and sacrifices before friends published it in France. I believe the title of that book was "*Before Night Falls*" by Reinaldo Arenas. LeeAndrew said that I should do the same and share my story with the world. I laughed and said that nobody would like to read my story and that Polish gays had already divided into three camps long time ago – one hates me, the other admires and the third doesn't give a damn. Yet, his American optimistic spirit shone through after my comment.

LeeAndrew glanced at me astonished and said: "*And who said that you should write it for the Poles? Write it for the world.*"

I thought for a few moments. Is the world really going to be interested in a Szymon Niemiec's story? Is anyone in far away in

America, France, England or Spain going to be interested in the lot of a Polish activist, who through a series of events and coincidences, was on the original frontlines for the LGBT movement in his country? I had many doubts. It was difficult to me to believe that my life may be interested to anyone. Of course, I'm used to the fact, that from time to time a journalist comes to me and asks me about various things gay related. But to be honest, they rarely ask me about my life. So, if nobody cares about my story in Poland, why on earth would anyone beyond Poland be interested in it?

Besides, the only thing I can do is to tell everything that I remember very subjectively. Certainly, many people will not like my version of events. Many will feel offended. Many will hate me for this. And again threats, corrections, sulks and criticism will begin. Why the hell should I do it? – I began asking myself. Wouldn't it be better to let the people forget about me? And let them live in a fallacious conviction that they know their version of the story, from which someone has erased my name very carefully? Is it worth going to another war for a book? I wasn't really sure.

When I was sharing this doubts with LeeAndrew, my black American friend looked at me with a serious expression on his face and said:"*Szymon, there are over150 nations in the world. In each of them there are homosexual people. And in some of those nations there was someone, who began a struggle for the rights of these people.* He continued as he often does, "*You belong to a few thousand of individuals who began something. This makes your story unique and worth telling. For this is a story of one individual among few.*"

I have never thought about it this way. It has always seemed to me, that I simply do what I think to be right. The fact that this brought about a change was amazing for me. But I accepted this as a kind of obviousness.

But LeeAndrew insisted. Every day at least once he mentioned a book, the story and that I should finally tell it. To put this delicately, I was beginning to be a bit irritated, so finally, for the sake of peace, I told him that I would try. No sooner had I told this than I started to regret my decision.

But I am the kind of man that doesn't like to breach my promises or not to meet commitments. Vision of writing my story was hanging over my head like a sword of an executioner over a convict and I knew that sooner or later I would have to sit at a computer and start to commit everything to paper. To write everything and remember details, sometimes even despite myself lack of motivation.

Okay, LeeAndrew you wanted a story. You'll have it. It is a story of a young man, who together with others initiated the homosexual movement in Poland. I was just a cog in a huge machine of human transformers. I was one of the first openly gay and identifiable, but not the only one. The book you have in your hands will not answer all your questions. It is not a lexicon of the Polish LGBT movement. I am not going to deprive historians of pleasure of describing everything their way. It is going to be an account of what I have seen and experienced in the way I was feeling and witnessed with my eyes and other senses.

In this experience I have come to realize that you only live once, despite others that perhaps wish otherwise.

In the first place, let's try to systemize and arrange it to make a neat whole. A key question, what to begin with?

Okay, perhaps without going too far. We are not going to make a fuss and tell old, worn out texts, let's start with my beginning. In the beginning there was nothing, except confusion but a sense and desires.

My family has never been one of the traditional, "normal" families of the times of the People's Republic of Poland. A strong public spirit accompanied us for generations. My grandparents were shop owners and lived with strict principles if fairness. Among other things, it was my Granddad, whose portrait hangs on my wall even today, who established the first cooperative "Dom Mody Astra" (Astra Fashion House) in Warsaw.

I think of him often and keep his portrait to look after me. Granddad was never a member of a communist party PZPR (Polish United Workers' Party) and had no connections with Russians; somehow he managed to create things, which constituted expressive freedom and motive d him.

A certain anecdote concerning this cooperative comes to my mind. Mody Astra was founded in the times when every enterprise that opened in Poland had to be named so that our „eastern friends" liked it. Thanks to this, picks like "Red Poppies", "Friendship" and so on was arising. Granddad strongly opposed naming the clothes cooperative „Red Star". Once he was at a meeting and he spotted a Soviet colonel treating somebody to cigarettes. These were equivalents of Marlboro, which were lacking those days and they were called "Astra", to honor something, though nobody remembered what. Granddad pondered a while and run to the bureau to submit and register a name "Astra Fashion House." When the officials suggested that the name should be more „patriotic", he answered with holy indignation insisting that he just wanted to honor a great soviet technical concept. Fancy, the sad men were convinced. Thanks to this, Astra has survived with the unchanged name and outlived all the meanders of history.

Generally, granddad was a great character. His office doors were always open for everyone. When he saw a weeping cleaning lady in a hallway, he stopped and asked what the problem was. The most often it would end in bringing the husband-drunkard to the office and offering him a job in hopes to drying-out him out. Everybody loved granddad.

When he died of cancer an estimated crowd of ten thousand people attended his funeral in Warsaw. Everybody was assuring solemnly that they would never forget the founder of the Astra, the Warszawianka, the Warsaw Cycling Association and other organizations. As it turned out, one year later, after his death, practically nobody came at the requiem mass.

Grandma was now ruling the kingdom, which was a villa in a beautiful district of Warsaw. "Sadyba" was our neighborhood and remains the place which I will always associate with greenery, peace and quietness. It is the place, where most of my childhood passed and after many years I came back here to find my special place on earth to remain. During their marriage my grandparents built a beautiful house, in which there was enough place for them, their parents, my mother, her sister and with time also for my father and me. We made up quite a harmonious family. Grandma devoted herself to her passion, which was dentistry, which also gained her admiration and respect of the whole neighborhood. I remember how she told me a story, how that an impressive limousine pulled up in front of our house and a woman Gypsy expensively dressed got out. It was probably one o'clock in the morning, when my Grandma opened the door to greet her. It came to be known that a local Gypsy king had suffered a terrible toothache, but his honor kept him from coming in person to visit a woman doctor. Grandma got dressed cursing silently and she went to his "palace" to relieve his suffering. She was completely stunned when later in the morning she discovered two fat geese on her doorstep.

Grandma mostly worked healing teeth of all the local drunkards and thieves and seldom received nice gifts like the geese as payment for services. Some people held a grudge against her for helping the less fortunate. However it was a good thing because I recall a particular Sunday a "someone" broke windows in all the villas in our street, but our house windows remained intact. Also, nothing ever vanished from our property. The local drunkard's and thief's honor didn't allow them to touch anything of friends. Eh, what happened to those times?

The Sadyba of those times was a real enclave of tolerance. I remember, that Grandma telling me about an old gay couple, who settled in a small house near the Czerniakowskie Lake and who came to her to heal their teeth. Everybody knew about them, but no one was making any problems. They were simply okay people. When the older one of them died, his partner was coming to my Grandma shearing his sorrow with tears. And he wasn't the only one who treated our house as an equivalent of a confessional box. Years were passing, people were changing.

**Someone saw you when you said
"Good Morning" to this gay!**

Sadyba was changing with them.

My mother met my father in a high school. Both were attending a prestigious Warsaw Stefan Batory High School. After high school finals, both started advanced studies. At first, my Father decided to study Polish philology, and mother economy. Two years later a wedding took place and my father changed his course of study and decided to study medicine. In January 1977 the two went to spend a holiday in the mountains. I suppose it was very cold during that holiday because some months later I would be born. Now you know, what my mad parents were doing on the peak of the mountain on a frosty January day, don't you?

But, if we want to follow the theory saying that life begins at the moment of conception, I think that I deserve the title of the youngest mountaineer...

I was there to see the place may years later, I was really impressed for I couldn't imagine how my Father had made Mother practice this kind of a method of "warming up in the frost" on such a narrow bed. Though, knowing my parents you could expect everything.

During mother's pregnancy she was working hard, having resigned from the pursuit of her education in favor of working at "Orion" Clothier Company. She provided keeping herself, her husband who was studying medicine and me in prospect. Physically her stomach didn't show too much during the beginning, so she didn't worry at all. Three days before the expected delivery she was coming back from Łódź as a transport escort. She was sitting next to a truck driver, a man of French descent. While they were driving back to Warsaw, one moment this nice foreigner pointing at my Mom's stomach said it was round as a ball. He also humorously noticed that probably not much time has left to the delivery. My Mother said calmly that she had perhaps three days remaining. We almost paid for this with life, because the shocked driver suddenly brought the vehicle to a stop and pulled over immediately. He stated that he was not going any further. He said that in France there was a ban in force forbidding pregnant women above the 6th month to work. Fortunately, my Mother's eloquence, or maybe her threat, that she would give birth to a child in his car convinced him and the journey continued without incident.

Three days later as foreseen, labor pains began. My grandparents were not home so my father called a taxi, which took them to the Czerniakowski Hospital. To this day, my mother recalls the moments while being driven in one of the last Warszawa cars in the capital, which was driven by an aged taxi driver. All the way he was trying to quiet down my mother repeating: "*Don't you worry, lady. So far it never happened that I have been late.*" They arrived at the hospital just in time.

My father, a medical student, insisted on being present at the delivery. No one could explain to him that it would be better if he waited in corridor. Finally, a clever obstetrician sent him to fetch a detail from the other end of the hospital. Before my father came back, everything was over.

While it is true that I got all the possible points given to a child at birth, but following the fact that my mother didn't have enough water, I was born with a distinctly flattened scull on one side. An orthopedist, who saw me a few days later, stated that I wouldn't develop normally and I would die soon or become a cripple. The poor fellow didn't know my folk and their determination in all things.

My grandma gave me enormous attention especially pinching my cheek and massaging temples patiently for many years, thanks to which she managed to smooth all the unevenness. But the first really serious problem was yet to come and it was deciding upon a name. Our two families almost split because of that. Grandmas on both sides were fighting stiffly for their rights. I was to be Kuba (Jacob) or Marcin (Martin). Any other version hadn't been taken into consideration at all. And because the both sides were deathly offended one at the other, none of them visited hospital. While a telegram came from my mother's parents: *"We are very happy for our grandchild. You can call him whatever you want, provided that you call him Kubuś"*.

If anyone wonders, from whom I inherited rebelliousness and stubbornness, I can safely say that from my father. With a crumpled telegram in his hand he came to the departmental nurse and asked her to enter the first name that came to his mind. It was Szymon (Simon). Grandma hadn't been able to forgive him that for a long time. But as it turned out later, this name fitted me like a glove.

The first years of my childhood I spent, of course, in Sadyba, in my grandparents' villa. I don't remember much from these times, but from what parents say, nobody had enough time to take care of me. Mother was working and studying, father was too, granddad was working and my grandma was spinning between the surgery and the kitchen.

Out of necessity, a nanny was hired to look after me. Though, there was someone, who had already taken care of me. My first protector was Nua, a 14-year-old German Shepherd female.

When I appeared in the house, this wonderful animal accepted me as a new pup in her pack and she took loving care of me. In the garden, which was her kingdom, I felt like the safest creature under the sun. But before I could start to get to know the beauty of the external world, another encounter with medicine was to be my experience.

In January 1978, to everybody's surprise, a minor cold turned into a double pneumonia for me. Practically, for a 3-month-old child in the 70s that diagnosis was equal to death sentence. An old doctor, who was called to see me, nodded sadly and she wrote a referral for me to be taken to the hospital. There wasn't much hope. In those times, infant mortality was huge. But I was lucky, because my father put his foot down and he didn't let me go to hospital.

Our home was transformed into a ward. In the attic, where we lived, wet sheets had been hung out, which were to help me to breathe. My parents were keeping vigil with me in their arms, because when they put me flat on my back, I was immediately beginning to choke. Every three hours I got a heroic dose of antibiotic medicines. Meanwhile, on the first floor, a war council of my grandparents and an aunt was taking place, because "this incompetent medical student wants to kill the child". But they didn't know either my father or me. Again, in defiance of the astonished doctor and all the predictions, I survived.

When finally my baby carriage could be put outside, Nua took care of me again. I was appropriated by her as her beloved pup and nobody except my grandma and mum could come up to me. It was just out of the question. In any case, Nua was an exceptional dog.

She hated two things. Cats and alcohol. No cat, which crosses the border of our garden, could survive. She was merciless. Only appearance of me in my baby carriage in the garden made her liberate her habits a bit. Though, she had never tolerated alcohol. Once when my granddad came home after one glass of vodka she runs to him to greet him, as usual. But when she smelled the alcohol, she moved back. She turned her back on him and she wouldn't go near him for a few following days. She ignored him to such an extent, that when he stood in her way in the doorway, she banged her head on his legs, and then passed round him and kept on going her way. No kind of bribery helped. She forgave him after a certain time.

When on warm days my baby carriage appeared in the backyard, instantly the garden was divided into several zones. The first zone, within a radius of 5 meters from my carriage was a zero zone. Only Nua, grandma and mum were allowed to enter it. Any other being could pay with their life for violating that border. Another zone was an area from 5 meters to the half of the garden. Other household members were allowed to stay there. The next was the third zone, in which during Nua's permitted cats to move freely. Nua protected me attentively. When I would cry, she used to raise the alarm for my family and the whole neighborhood. When I slept for too long, she was hopping on two legs to see of I was all right in my baby carriage. Imagine a nearly two meters long dog hopping on two legs next to a baby carriage. This had to be a sweet sight.

Nua's control came to an end, when I began to crawl. Her beloved pup started to rummage the garden and she didn't know what to do. I was lacking a skin fold on my neck, which she could grab with her muzzle and bring me back home. Finally, she limited herself to following me with her nose next to my diaper and she turned me back with her muzzle when I went away too far, in her opinion. She allowed me for much. Grandma told me, that one day she left the house and in the instant of her return she got rooted to the spot with terror. She saw the dog sitting with the muzzle open and her grandchild keeping his hand immersed in the dog's throat up to his elbow. Reportedly, Nua looked at my grandma with her eyes saying: "What should I have done?" In any case, she had never hurt me in any way. And she never let anyone hurt me. Once, when someone raised his hand against me for fun, instantly Nua was at his throat and my father and granddad had to intervene to save the joker's life. From that moment, nobody ever had been kidding in this way.

We were in tears mourning for her, when Nua had to be put to sleep. She was 18 years old and she seriously suffered from nasal. Toward the end of her life, she was nearly blind and she couldn't walk. But when she scented me, at once she started to pretend, that she was all right and she was ready to play. She was the most faithful protector that I ever had.

After Nua, Rambo came. He was a young German Shepherd, an exact opposite of her. This young, spoiled by everybody animal was chasing everything that moved. He didn't despise any human, whose face could be licked off. And he loved my mother's lap. I remember when he, being already quite a mature dog, still loved to climb her lap. Usually, that looked in this way, that his three legs fit, but the fourth one was hanging from my mother's knees successively destroying her every next new panty-hoses. And you must know that in those times, panty-hoses were goods remarkably in short supply. Having a crazy dog, my granddad felt motivated to reorganize the garden. Consequently, new gates, wood and wire fences appeared. But you are wrong, if you think that any fence could stop him from greeting every patient visiting grandmother. With time, the doggie grew prosperous and got a brick kennel, where he lived happily to the end of his life. He was let out only after the surgery had been closed, to allow him to romp freely in the garden.

My grandparents' garden my granddads greatest joy he was very proud of it, for there were many plants, that were unique examples in Warsaw. Apart from the botanical gardens, we had two beautiful specimen of edible chestnut. Granddad was also growing pears, apples, raspberries, currants and even peaches and apricots. In a distant corner of the garden, there was an eternally shady realm of grapevine. I remember those juices, jellies and jams made of the grapes by grandmother.

I don't remember much from that first stage of my life, but from what my mother tells me, and from flashes of my own memory, I know that there were two places, where they always could look for me and they found me. The garden was the first where I had my secret hiding places and hideouts. I spent most time there, which drove my baby-sitters, grandma and mum to despair, for they spent long hours looking for me not being able to find me in the jungle of a raspberry grove, which occupied three quarters of the whole garden.

Though experienced trackers knew well, that there was a clearing in the middle of the thicket, where I used to lie down to have a nap after dinner. In the garden there was also a shed with a garage. I used to hone my inventor talents there. I must admit, that my granddad and grandma were supporting me in that, hoping that maybe some day I would become an engineer.

When I was 11, my mother coming home saw grandma carrying a heavy plank. She asked her, what she was doing and she heard a serious answer: *"Szymek is building a glider."* To tell you the truth, I have never finished my plane, but at least I have tried.

If I weren't in the garden, because of bad weather or cold, you could find me in the kitchen. There, under supervision of grandma and sometimes also father, I was getting to know many secrets of culinary arts.

Oh, the kitchen at Goraszewska Street... Grandma's secret notes writ also written on a yellowed notebook and long stories such as the superiority of a yeast cake over layer shortcake.   Anyway, my love for cooking remains to this day.

I don't remember exactly, when my parents decided to become self-dependent.   Anyway, it didn't affect my life too much, for we still used to spend every weekend in Sadyba.   Though, our official place of living became Warsaw Ursynów, precisely the eleventh floor of a new high-rise building in Puszczyka Street. It was a perfect location, for it had a great bus connection with the center, a special convenience for my mother in the form of a day care center, a nursery school and a school just next to our apartment house. And for me, it was a luxury because I got my own room.

I remember my first babysitter on Ursynów. She was a young daughter of our neighbors. One day we painted together the whole wall of my room with crayons. These were beautiful times, sometimes brutally interrupted with a minor refitting and with a wallpaper of bamboo pattern, in which you couldn't draw.

In the meantime, I was sent to a day care center. I remember that establishment only because of an image of women tutors bringing huge kettles filled with whey, which they served us, hoping that this filth would improve our health. Also then, my visits to my father's family in the area of Białystok began. The White Primeval Forest in the Rabalina village is where my adventures with discovering the true beauty of nature. Maybe you will think that it's strange, but thanks to those visits I started to appreciate quality food. My grandma, in spite of her wonderful cuisine, couldn't make me eat. I preferred to cook than to eat. I still have a picture of me sitting on a working washing machine, a burning candle in the background and my grandma, who was trying to feed me. Believe it or not, it wasn't easy to make me eat.

Finally, my father, being a severe physician, discovered a solution. We were on vacation in Rabalina village. He asked me, if I wanted to have breakfast. Of course, the answer couldn't be different. "No." And that's it. "OK," my father said, and he took me for a 4 hour walk in the forest. When we got home, he asked me, if I wanted to have lunch. Again, I refused. So father didn't persuade me and he took me for another 4 hour long walk to the forest. After we came back home, I myself asked my aunt, what we were going to have for dinner. That made her really happy.

Anyway, in that way I got to know a wonderful taste of kartacze, potato dumpling, stiffed with venison. Their taste can't be replaced with anything else. It took me 14 years to get a recipe for that dish. I will share it with you some time. Many years of visits to Rabalina and Ełk, where my second grandma lived, bore fruit in the form of even bigger attachment to culinary arts and nature and an inestimable dose of eastern madness. Grandma Jadzia, as opposed to Warsaw grandma Wandzia, was not a staid matron.

When I was still a little boy, grandma Jadzia was working as a principal of a high school in Ełk. In those times, you could go to jail for making wine for your personal use. Though, from time to tome my grandma was sending us a parcel with four jars. The jars were filled with home made spirits. How did she secure the content against a government postal control? On each of the jar there was a label saying

"Holy water." Grandma fervently believed that communists were afraid of holy water and they wouldn't touch the parcel. Apparently, she must have been correct.

After many years, I got to know, that my grandma was a real eccentric. She distilled the spirit in her office in school. Why didn't she ever have any problems with the authorities? Perhaps it was because she was a principal, whom everybody loved. Father told me that once during high school finals, when she was a member of an examining board, a girl coming to return her work, dropped her papers while approaching the desk. In those times, there was a rule in schools, that if the chairman of the examining board didn't notice anything, there was no problem with examination. At the exam, grandma ran to the window to admire the weather, while the girl took her papers from the floor hastily. This was my grandma.

But not only had my father's side overflowed in madness and extraordinary ideas. Mother told me a story about our attendance at a wedding in her mother's (and my grandma's) home village. Everything was prepared for the wedding party, which was going to be held the next day. There were many types and kinds of cakes.

Unfortunately, one of the uncles had a nap in this room. He slept soundly and loudly. His snoring could be heard in the whole house. I was so much alarmed with that sound, that I ran to my aunt with terror and I asked her if uncle wasn't going to "snore off" the cakes. They've reminded me that to this day. I recall another interesting visit spending a few summers holidays in that village called

Ciechomin. It was there I got to know martial arts against chickens. Yes, yes. Don't laugh at me. An aggressive rooster could be a serious opponent for a 4-year-old kid. Once I was attacked by this chicken leader in the courtyard, I was defending myself bravely with a stick till grandma came to my rescue. For me the story ended with a scratched face while for the rooster it ended with a broth. In this charming country seat I also discovered a secret kept by chickens very well. If you could see my face when I saw in dismay that they could fly that is how "Grandpa Chicken on The Roof" became my nickname for the next few years.

Another place, where we spent holidays was a seaside village Kąty Rybackie, where granddad built a gorgeous resort for his workers. Of course, as we were the president's family, the rooms were always ready waiting for us. From those times I remember taste of freshly smoked fish, crawfish being boiled in the middle of the night and a cathedral in Oliwa very well.

During one of these visits to the seaside, my father was serving 3 months of an accelerated military service. Later he confessed that most of that time he spent in custody for "causing the platoon go cheerful." At the military oath rite I made my mother feel very ashamed, for when I saw recruits getting off a delivery van Star, I yelled at the top of my voice: "Mother, look... so many dads!" Apparently I was already attracted to men in military uniform.

While on breaks and between holidays and weekend stays on Sadyba I was leading a normal life of a happy kid. Okay, maybe it wasn't too normal. For example, not every kid has a chance to greet his father who arrived home for dinner in an ambulance with the siren blaring. This was exciting for me. Dad was working for the emergency service, making up for duties that he needed for further education. I remember he was telling us about one of his favorite patients she was an elderly lady with a serious hyperacidity, who loves sauerkraut stew with meat. She was old and experienced, so she knew the timing and abilities of medical care system and she was usually calling for ambulance at the moment when the dish was nearing to be ready. Before the ambulance appeared, the elderly lady had already her stew and had been waiting for the ache and medications. Though once she failed because my father hit up on a sly idea and he came to her quicker than usual. Perplexed the old lady managed only to spit out," *My dear! But I didn't have time to eat.*" No excuses were of any help and the lady landed up in hospital, just preventively.

I too had foods that I liked and disliked. My hatred for spinach and mushrooms started in nursery school one day when they gave us mushroom stewed sautéed in butter. I remember vomiting really heavily after eating it. We never got to know, what was wrong with it. One day mother, who didn't know about the previous school incident, nearly did me in with another helping of stewed mushroom, which spontaneously left my stomach the same way that it entered. I learned to like this delicious mushroom many years later, after I had left primary school.

The schools made spinach disgusting for me when I was a kid; they used to feed us in Polish nursery schools with an insipid pulp with no salt, pepper or garlic, but with fried eggs.

I started to like spinach only, when I was student at a college. However as for fried eggs, I've been repelled by it up to this day.

My culinary memories from childhood wouldn't be complete without two more anecdotes. The first one concerns the times, when we just moved into our flat on Ursynów.

My mother was just learning to cook and not everything she made was edible. We still laugh remembering her first fruit-filled dumplings.
Definitely, fruit-filled dumplings are vicious dish to make for a beginner cook. But my mother was stubborn and wanted to make them by herself. Anyway, the dumplings appeared to be "shell-proof."

We lived on the 11th floor, so the final test for the dumplings, after we had tried to get inside, to a plum, with a knife, was dropping them down to the ground from the window.
Maybe it's difficult to believe, but the next day we found the dumplings slightly flattened lying on the ground. We've laughed for a long time at those dumplings, my mother eventually learned to cook them properly. Though, I must admit, that our whole family still prefer to buy dumplings at a grocery store.

My father's inclination to experiment with home production of various beverages also held memories. I remember that in our kitchen there was always something strange looking was quietly about.

Because there were five apple trees in my grandparents' garden, some of them always were being processed. Once my father decided to make cider but unfortunately this particular batch turned sour. Father wasn't in the habit of wasting anything, so he decided to transform the unsuccessful beverage into apple vinegar – great for various salads and pickles. Thus, the soured concoction was left to mature in the kitchen. Nobody knows if the event was provoked by a latent defect of the glass container or maybe mum pressed the container against the floor finish too strongly while moving it. Anyway, one night, a terrible bang woke us up, as if our entire block was falling down. Horrified neighbors started to knock on our door and we got into panic and started to look for the source of the explosion.

When we entered the kitchen, we saw… an apple Armageddon. The 15-litre glass container filled with 10 liters of fermented and soured apples simply blew up. An unbearable smell of apple vinegar had been wafting in the kitchen for many weeks, and seeds and rinds were found in draws closed tightly and even after a few years.

This scary experience however had a good side effect. It turned out, that our vinegar bomb caused our flat was free from pest of housing of those days, the dreaded Pharaoh ants. Those clever creatures for no particular reason simply hated the scent of vinegar.

To tell the truth, to this day my mum has claimed that it was a wild rose wine, and I don't know, why in my memory these were apples. Maybe my grandparents' apple trees influenced me so much or maybe it was a mysterious disappearance of the ants?

Anyway, Pharaoh ants it is a yet a different story. Everyone living in a block of flats in the 80s knew exactly what they are. They were a real modern day plague. They could come from nowhere and take control over an entire flat. They literally would control every square meter. The ants were infamous to morning coffee drinkers, a sugar bowl played host to any family of ants who are carrying sugar particles out constantly.

Together with my neighbors' children we were making experiments arranging fruit pieces in the middle of a patter filled with water, and building many bridges made of matches. We were watching the ants sending their scouts, who were looking for the way to get to the fruit. We were very happy, when they chose one the ways built by us, though sometimes they took us by surprise.

In the village of Ursynów, my christening was held, as well. I was baptized a little bit later than it usually happens, but that was because of my father's unbending character and an equally unbending character of the parson in the parish, where my grandparents lived.

**I know that Our Lord is always right, but when
I am thinking that I should live with my own rib...**

I know from stories, that right after my birth, my grandparents began to arrange my baptism. Though, the parson wanted my father – already known to be an atheist - to visit him. The parson was trying to convince my father to return to the bosom of the Roman Catholic Church.

They say, that it ended with slamming of the vestry door and my father's statement, that the child was not going to be baptized at all, unless over his dead body.

As it turned out my father didn't have to die and I was baptized as the eldest child in a group, in the basement of a church being constructed then in Ursynów. To the parish on Sadyba, I returned not before I moved back to the grandparents' home.

In Poland, a child up to being seven-year old stays in the custody of the parents or he or she takes advantage of a nursery school, either public or private. At least, this happens at present. Though, when I was a child, the parents didn't have much choice. Practically, there were no private nursery schools and rarely people could afford a twenty-four-hour baby-sitter. Thus, I landed in two Ursynów nursery schools subsequently. The first one was a public nursery school located in the neighborhood of the Horse Races. This respectable establishment was located in a beautiful old building. I didn't attend it for too long, but I remember very well, that that nursery school had its own stage. That was the place where I experienced the taste of acting, starring as a cat. Mum told me, that at nights she was making me a costume according to the lady teachers' directions.

Anyway, mum had always been skillful with hands and she made me many costumes for many various carnival balls.

After a short adventure with a nursery school at Wyścigowa Street, I landed in another one, which was located just next to our block of flats. For me, that was a totally different world. This meant new building, new friends, and new teachers. Interestingly enough, I already then appeared to be an individualist and didn't want to adept myself to the standards which were binding then. Instead of changing groups with time, like every normal child did, I was changing them at random. Most of the time I was spending with the oldest kids, for my peers didn't suit me. Or maybe rather it was me, who didn't suit them.

When I look at myself as a child from a perspective of my experience today, I can say I was growing up to be a homosexual. As one and the only boy in the nursery school I wasn't interested in football, cars or soldiers. Whereas I was studying cooking passionately and I was the first one in the group who got his own mini kitchen. It may sound funny, but that toy mini kitchen cost a fortune and you could get it only in one shop in the whole city.

I still feel moved, when I think of it, though my mum says, that I had been playing with it for only one week.

And it turned out already then, that there was someone, who noticed that I wasn't going to grow a normal child. One day, a school lady educator called my father to come and talk about me seriously. A certain event aroused her serious concern for me. Few days before, a lady with a cello gave a concert at our nursery school.

These kind of musical meetings were supposed to have a good effect on children. Of course, most of my peers was doing everything but listening during the concert. Except for me. According to the disturbed lady educator, during the entire concert I was sitting calmly and listening to the music attentively. Because of this concentration, I didn't even noticed, that I put a slipper into my mouth. The teacher stated that that was a bad sign.

Unfortunately, she wasn't so lucky because she met my father, who had his own opinion on educators. Again, the door slammed but this time I stayed in the nursery school.

According to the rules of education, a child should leave the nursery school with the knowledge of at least the block letters of the alphabet. We were learning it form an ABC book and we used bricks with letters. That is, all the other kids were learning letters in that way. Because I was learning how to read from comic books featuring Kajko and Kokosz. When my father noticed, that I was quite good at reading he started to devote a part of the evening for reading my first book with me. That was "Schwambranien" by Lew Kassil. This autobiographic novel from the times of the First World War opened the door to imagination in front of me. You know that kids have a great imagination, right? I could sit in my room alone and for hours study my own internal world, which I had created myself.

When we finished reading "Schwambranien," it turned out that I can read by myself quite fluently. My father threw me at the deep end giving me the first volume of Tolkien's trilogy to read. This was my first book, that I read totally unassisted. Then, many other books came.

I can proudly say that I've been devouring books to this day. As a five-year old kid, I had read three volumes of "The Lord of the Rings" in two weeks. Later on, I took up other readings. Father says, that he was most surprised when he entered his study and saw me leaning over a anatomic atlas. I didn't understand a word, but out of habit I was reading anything within my reach.

When I was finally finishing the advanced group and preparing to attend the 1 f class of the primary school located next to the nursery school, my granddad fell ill. It turned out, that he had a palatal cancer and needed permanent medical assistance. At that time, my parents decided to move back to Sadyba to enable my father help grandma in care over granddad. I was to go to the 1 a class of the Heroes of Warsaw Primary School No 103. I didn't know then, that I was going to spend there the most interesting and the most stressing 8 years of my life.

Though, we all believed, that we would manage to overcome my granddad's disease. God knows how much wrong we were.

At first, we moved to the attic in the second half of the house. The second floor was taken absolutely by my great-grandmother. Till her last days she had been telling colorful stories from the times of the First and the Second World War up to her last days. She taught me ecumenism by telling me stories about hiding Jews and an Orthodox icon saved from the soviets.

I will always associate my great-grandmother with one more thing that was a peculiar, never ending fight with her daughter-in-law that was my grandma. Since great-grandmother Irena was in a strange habit from the times of two world wars.
She lived in a continuous fear that war might break again any moment. That's why she was collecting bread all her life busily. She was buying huge amounts of bread loafs, she cut them into slices, she dried them in the stove and she hid them inside a pillow case that was in the wardrobe. Twice a year, my grandma stole that pillow case from the wardrobe and she threw the dry bread to a garbage can. My great-grandmother used to make a wild scene and she started the whole procedure from the very beginning.

My father transformed a garage that was located under a huge porch into his first consulting-room. Also then, for the first time, I wasn't allowed to play in the garden when he was working. Father must have been afraid, that I would spy on him through the window. Though, he didn't suspect that I knew his consulting-room very well, because when he was going away, I used to "borrow" the keys and I rummage that room, which strangely smelled with disinfectants. I knew exactly every tool and device in the consulting-room. I was always curious.

Granddad was working most of the time of his illness. When successive operations didn't take any effect, he was slowly withdrawing from his duties. The last operation took his voice away, and it made working impossible for him. He isolated himself at home and he began to die.

Though, before that happened we managed to celebrate my aunt's wedding (who then moved to her husband's, to the seaside), and my first Holy Communion, for which I got a bicycle. In those times, I used to love clogs. Those shoes with wooden sole were my favorite footwear.

Guess what shoes I was wearing at my first bicycle ride. It ended happily probably only because it didn't take too long.

But before the first Holy Communion, I went to school.

This wouldn't be me, if it was just normal.

In the 1 a class, I had stayed only for one year. Unfortunately, I don't remember what were the reasons, why to the second class I was attending with a group with the letter d instead of a. Today I must admit it wasn't quite a fortunate coincidence.

Being a stranger, I was always standing aside. I was going to church and I even became an altar boy. Though soon, I resigned as an altar boy because I constantly saw nuns stealing gifts from the USA care packages.

When I was ten, my mother sent me for the first winter holiday camp in my life. Granddad, who was already immobile at that time, and had to be fed through a nasal probe, insisted on my going very much. Apparently, he sensed coming death. He passed away two days after I had left. That's why I didn't have a chance to be present at his funeral. When I came back and they told me what happened, my despair was no end.

Though, soon it turned out that my Granddad hadn't left me all alone. Still the same year, on a warm day we went for a two-day trip to the Kampinos Forest. Something happened, that made me look at the extrasensory world much more attentively.

Already then, I was treated as a stranger in my peers' group. I was more mature, well-read and I preferred discussing with teachers than to playing football.

On that trip we were to sleep in typical summer houses. Those were triangular buildings, in which the rooms were located according to the same scheme. Downstairs there was a four person's room; upstairs there were two rooms, a single and a double one. You can easily guess which of the rooms happened to be mine.

After darkness had fallen, I left the building to wash myself in a common bathroom, which was situated in a separate building. It was a warm, cloudless night. When I finished washing my teeth and I was going to leave, in a corridor I saw my Granddad, who was sitting on a chair and he was shaking his finger at me with a severe or maybe sad face.

As you may expect of a ten-year-old boy, I started to scream and I rushed into our house terror-struck. When I told the rest of the children, what happened, it led to the situation that nearly our whole class slept in one four-man room. In the middle of that night, a terrible storm blew up. One of the thunders hit a tree next to our house and broke a branch, which broke the window-pane and thrust into the bed, in which I was supposed to sleep. I've claimed since that my Granddad had saved my life.

After my Granddad's death, we moved from the great-grandmother's attic to the other side of the house. Dad occupied Granddad's study. He continued his learning within the breaks between emergency services. Mum reined the attic; I had my duchy in front of my dad's study. It was my mother's old room. Even the furniture was the same. These were one of the first furniture you could assemble by yourself at home. That was one of the wonders of technology of those days. They were falling apart constantly but they were what we had.

Next to my room, there was a bathroom with a brick shower cabin, a huge tub, a water closet and a bidet. Everything was tiled in white.

In that bathroom, thanks to my father I leaned the beauty of photography. This is where my first darkroom was located. My mother has preserved all the photographs from those times. Now and then, I like to go back to them.

I didn't suspect that a cloud was on the horizon for my whole family. Everything seemed to shape up well. Though my parents didn't devote too much time to me, because they were busy with their work, they were trying to take me for holidays abroad at least once a year. Thanks to that I got to know many foreign countries.

Especially, I remember two trips, to Egypt and Bulgaria. To the first of those two countries we went by plane. Those six hours of flight were really something. For a child of my age, all those pressure changes, a wonder of technology in the form of an airplane, and nervous waiting to see a country which I knew only from books and films – all that was extraordinary.

I remember my first encounter with the African land very well. We were welcomed already in the open door of the plane with a wall of difficult to breathe air. Hot, soaked through with the scent of the ground, spices and the Nile River, the air gave us little chance to take a deep breath. We landed at night, but the temperature in Cairo didn't fall below 104° F. It soon appeared that at day it was even warmer.

Before we came to a flat, in which we were to stay, and which belonged to my godfather, at whose invitation we came there, we popped in a duty free shop. And after the shopping, we left for our lodgings supplied with high-proof spirit bottles. But my mum made a cardinal mistake and gave me a bag with the bottles.

Of course, I had to fall down and break everything just in the door of the flat. I don't know who was more embittered, me or my godparents. Anyway, the next day in the corridor we met a group of Cairo men, who were inhaling the alcohol vapors with delight, because they were not allowed to drink it.

In Egypt, I got to know the taste of real ice creams. Later I hadn't been able to find it anywhere in the world for many years. In those times in Poland, there were only vanilla ice creams on sticks called Bambino and ice cream blocks available in the ice cream shops. Also, I learned what meant a rule of a concern for family. For Muslims, I was a child, so I was to be protected, regardless of the fact that I was infidel. That's why nobody ever hurt me there, even when I was walking alone on an Arab market. Finally, mum started to send me to do shopping at a bakery, for it turned out that a small child could communicate with the baker in Polish easier that a grown-up in English. I still remember the taste of pancakes, which we called a "beret." They were baked of wheat-flour and constituted a basic food for the poor. When filled with meat and vegetable, they tasted better than a hamburger.

Egypt enchanted me with its culture, history and its amazing attitude towards tradition. That country nearly made my godfather an owner of a dozen camels and me a half-orphan. Cause during our visit to camel fair, one of the merchants offered 12 camels, including a white one to him for my mother. Fortunately, they didn't strike a bargain.

From Egypt I had brought many exhibits, most of which today decorates geographic and biologic classrooms in my primary school. Apart from that, I bought two desert turtles. Don't ask me how I did it. That was the first act of smuggling in my life.

The next journey that is still in my memory was a trip to Bulgaria. As opposed to the previous outing, we got by train to that warm climate country, which was under the reign of communist party in those times.

In order to spend two weeks in that "socialist heaven" we were traveling two days through all the possible countries. I remember Romania the most and a sight of children standing on a railway track and begging for anything to eat. We were throwing them everything sandwiches, pastries, and candies. Really everything.

In Bulgaria I learned two things. The first one was a siesta. For Bulgarians, between 12 and 14 was sacred and nobody was either working or going to the beach then. Everyone was hiding at home. We couldn't understand why until we went to a beach around 1 pm. We didn't reach the water. The sand mixed with black charcoal particles was very hot, that it was simply impossible to walk through it even in our flip-flops.

The second thing that Bulgaria taught me was an absolute ban on covering anything over the beach sand. And that concerned especially watermelons, which you could buy there at almost every corner.
Do you know why? A watermelon covered with the beach sand turns into a soup after an hour.

That journey was the last one that we made all together as a family. Soon, my father went away to England for a period of special medical training. He was sending me letters and once he even sent me the first computer in my life. I can assure the young generation, which surely don't remember the times, when computers were different than our PC, that Atari 65XE was the biggest dream of a child. I still remember 45 minutes of pious waiting to finish recording a game from a cassette recorder to a computer. In the game, circles looked quite square and the sound didn't match the present-day clock melodies. I could spend 6 hours in front of the computer and patiently, line by line, enter a code of a program and the only task of which was to display the American flag in the screen. Let's say, that the flag was a billowing delicately. Let's add to that a black-and white screen and a joystick breaking down continuously. Can you believe me, that then it was a state-of-the-art technology in Poland?

After my father had returned from the training, it was getting worst between my parents. Finally, they decided to get a divorce. This was the most difficult and traumatic experience of my childhood. I remember that when I was at a scout camp and I knew that my parents were going to get divorce, I was planning a great preventing operation. I wanted to come back to Warsaw, go to the court and tell the judges, that I didn't agree. I had spent most of those holidays crying. Though, the most painful for me was the way I got to know about their parting. It was at a lunch, one of the first lunches after the vacations. I remember, that I said that I would never agree to their divorce and I was going to go the court to tell them that.

My mum looked at me and said: "*But we got divorced 3 moths ago.*" That was a blow and I couldn't have pulled myself together for a long time. My education and whole life had suffered because of that. I hadn't been able to forgive my parents that they had decided to get divorced for many years. Both grannies added fuel to the flames. Unfortunately, I must admit it now, that for both of them it was a point of honor to convince an adolescent kid that it had been fault of the other side. Granny Wandzia was trying to convince me, that it had been my father's fault, while granny Jadzia was blaming my mum. I was torn between the two families and I had almost paid for it with sanity. Though, I managed to find a way to work the problem through. Theatre proved to be my salvation.

At those times, I was regularly playing at a school theatre and on my record I had a very successful debut as Papkin in "The Revenge" by Fredro. Though, I didn't think seriously about acting. I was captivated by a spiritual life and I wanted to become a priest. But just then, one of my biggest enemies, the man about which I will soon tell you, got to a Children Theatrical Center at the Ochota Theatre in Warsaw. He was boosting about that fact continuously, so it evoked a wild defiance in me. If he could do that – I thought to myself – why couldn't I?

I had passed my exams to the theatrical center splendidly, though my mum had paid for it with a broken tooth. It turned out that nuts topped with chocolate may be dangerous.

Anyway, I got to the 1 year of theatrical department led by a couple of wonderful actors and educators that was Halina and Jan Machulski.

To add to my happiness, the tutor of my group appeared to be Zofia Białoskórska. The fate was to connect me with her for many years. Theatre absorbed me completely. Although we had classes only once a week, for me they constituted a real escape and a refuge form the external world, the world, in which not many good things were happening.

My mum deprived of my granddad's help and totally broken down after the divorce with my father didn't have either time or energy to devote enough attention to me. That was why I had to learn to cope with life by myself. My class, my peers around me didn't make it easier, by no means. There were three people, whom I will remember till the end of my life. Their faces will haut me till death; Wojtek, Przemek and Sebastian. Those three kids from my class made up a real trio of hell. They tormented everyone who was weaker. Guess, who was their favorite victim? Though, I have to admit, that I myself was giving them cause for hatred.

I was different; I stood out among the rest. I was more sensitive, in love with poetry, I hated sports. In addition to that, I had a diagnosed dyslexia and IQ higher than theirs by a few points. As well, that dyslexia caused a lasting hatred between me and our teacher of Polish. Once, during a lesson, when she was giving us back our compositions, she stated that they should put kids like me in a mental institution. I had never forgiven her that.

Anyway, primary school for me was a number of consecutive acts of my humiliation. I recall with a shame, the time when I had tried to win favor of the devilish trio. I even went as far as inviting them to my home and letting them watch my father's porn cassette, which I had found in a wardrobe. Of course, my mum caught us watching and I got a pretty good scolding. I incurred most serious displeasure of those three monsters, when at a memorable history lesson I dared to say that I admired Jews. Those three young nationalists poured water on my head first having it put in a closet.

I'll never forget that at after that scandal, Wojtek's mum, in passing, a police officer responsible for juvenile delinquency department, stated that it was my fault, because I provoked her poor little child, who had to defend himself.

Basically, I've always had better relations with girls. Among boys, I become friends with Bartek – a young and very talented football player, Błażej, who was very fond of ancient history, as I did, and Michał – a grandchild of a famous writer, who was called the class swot.

After years, Bartek was the one, who disappointed me the most. He was the only person, who at the class meeting didn't shake hand with me and treated me with disgust. With Michał I maintain an occasional contact. Many years later, in 2001 he made a short documentary film about me, which must be lying somewhere in the archives of the Łódź Film School. What happened to the rest of them? I have no idea.

Many of them have left the country; some of them set in order their lives. Our paths have parted. And to be honest, I haven't maintained any contact with anybody from those times, except Aśka, at whom I was making a pass, and her brother.

Anyway, I've been always trying to erase those times from memories. I escaped to theatre. The world of stage absorbed me completely. I could get totally lost in it. In the middle of the first year of the theatrical department, Miss Białoskórska invited me to a rehearsal of a children and youth cabaret, which she was running in a local club called "Thirteen." In that way, I found a place, which appeared to be my home for the next ten years. "Lucky Thirteen" was something amazing. Step by step, a group of local kids was becoming a professional actors group under a watchful and loving eye of Miss Zosia. We wrote texts and songs by ourselves. Miss Zosia was accompanying us and helping us as she could. With time, I started to treat her as my theatrical mum. Those were really beautiful times. All the year we were working diligently over an artistic program, which then we presented at a Wola Overview of Amateur Artistic Groups. I don't know, if you will believe me, but after 4 years of our group winning the first awards, the board came to a conclusion that they had to create a separate contest category, because our programs were simply too good. Anyway, at that overview I got my first stage award. For 10 years I had been one of the authors of the cabaret. Also there I met my first love, Iwona, and my first best friend - Michał.

There are two more stories that I remember from the times of my primary school. The first one concerned my travel by boat through Dniestr River. That was a great two weeks trip through the half of the territory of the Soviet Union. It was great and unforgettable also because of a certain adventure in a town, where I was robbed of chewing gum. Also then, a love affair between mum and her present partner, Adam, began. He was then a head of the passport department. Thanks to him, I managed to get the passport quicker and to set out for an expedition. I remember my mother preparing me for Adam's first visit at our home. I was terribly excited and I asked her if I should call him "father." Mum wasn't sure what to answer, but Adam solved the problem at once and asked me to call him by his first name.

The second story related to the primary school was our class trip to Prague in Czechoslovakia. We went there in care of my mum and Adam exactly. Thanks to that trip, I learned to distinguish a good beer from a small beer. And I was promoted to be the class paramedic saving my school friends, who had a headache caused "by the wind."

Apart from theatre, I was trying to find my place on earth through the scout movement. Being a member of a group, which accepted me, allowed me to develop myself, and gave me an extension of a family, was a great help to me, a kid.

My first scout camp fell on the famous in Poland propaganda action called Bieszczady 40. That was one of the last great propaganda actions, during which they sent thousands of scouts to the Polish mountains in order to build a tourist centers. These camps were called labor camps, for practically they were free, but we had to work off the costs of our stay. My team, which consisted mostly of younger children, was sent to help farmers with their work. We were turning over hay in the field. That was a wonderful way of hardening our bodies and characters. In front of my eyes, I can still see a farmer giving us earthenware filled with sour milk and pieces of beeswax straight from beehives and homemade bread with butter. The taste of that meal that we got after a hard all-day work was refreshing.

Also in Bieszczady, I experienced first tornado in my life. That was a memorable night, when the whirlwind, a phenomenon very rare in Poland, went through Bieszczady and blew over a hundred-year-old oak tree in Łańcut. Our campsite was located 5 kilometers from the center of one of those whirlwinds.

At night, I saw the girls' heavy military tents flying in the air. The girls have fixed them to the ground not correctly. Later, we were finding their mess-tins deep in the forest.

I received my scout cross in Kopalin, a small resort at the Polish seaside during the camp, when my parent's divorce was hanging in the balance. These were the times, when a scout decided by himself if he wanted to pledge to God and Poland or to Poland only.

I quit scouting years later, at high school, when this respectable organization became an association of a religious character. Before that happened, I managed to experience an adventure with a parachuting team and my own theatrical team.

Anyway, high school was a very significant part of my growing up to who I am today.

A great dream of my mums was to own a home. Adam, a man fostered by tough country life, who bestowed a really passionate affection upon my mum, decided to fulfill her dreams. During one of their numerous excursions through the Polish villages, they came across two beautiful peasant huts made of larch that were for sale. Both were quite small, but in an exceptionally good condition. At that point, Adam's perfect household instinct took action and he found a man in that village in Poznań region, who built those huts with his sons. That craftsman together with his two sons undertook a difficult task to take the two huts to pieces and assemble one in Warsaw. At the moment, I owe you an explanation, that thanks to granddad's efforts, our family owned a patch of land on the other side of Vistula River. After long-lasting negotiations with the family, mum got the right to build her dreamed-of house on that terrain. When one winter day I saw four piles of larch wood lying on the ground covered with snow, I couldn't believe that some day it would constitute a genuine house. Though, Adam appeared to be a man who can turn dreams into actions. Again, thanks to him I had a chance to experience hard physical work. Together with an old carpenter and his two sons we were building our own common house. We still laugh, when recollecting an anecdote about the old carpenter, who asked Adam if he had a construction plan. Adam answered, that certainly, he had. He grabbed a piece of a cardboard and draw a picture of a hut with a pencil. That piece of cardboard served as a final construction plan till the end of building. Adam passed to me the secrets of peasant hut constructing. Thanks to him I got to know, that you should throw small change coins into wood frame foundations, which is the first wooden beams that they put on the brick fundament, to make the money always comes to the house owners. It was Adam, who also taught me a difficult trick to stick oakum into the walls and to paint the beams with burnt motor oil, which was to protect the walls from pests. Though, the moment of cutting the wooden frame foundations made the biggest impression on me.

Imagine my great surprise, when from seventy-year-old logs cut down to suit the proper size, resin started to drip. The old man, who was superintending his sons, explained to me patiently, that that indicated that the wood had been well preserved and our house would stand for more 70 years with no need of special repair. When the house was finally built, and we could practically move in, I just graduated primary school and it was the time to choose a high school.

At that time, the first of later many conflicts with my father arose. Father just couldn't understand why I didn't want to apply for the Batory. Cause in his head, there was still an idea that I should follow in his footsteps. Unfortunately, with my poor results at Polish, I couldn't even think about getting to the most prestigious high school in Poland.

Instead, I applied for the Adam Mickiewicz High School, which was located not far from our new home.

Though still, my handwriting placed me outside of any classification and after a repeat of a Polish exam, everything pointed at a threat of me landing at a vocational school. Fortunately, in our family there was Adam.

I don't know what arguments he used in his conversation with an old friend of his but it achieved something. Mum mentioned incidentally something about a bottle of good vodka, but I don't know, if that was the whole truth. And to be honest, I suppose, I don't quite want to know.

Anyway, I became a student of the 72th High School on the Warsaw Praga. I entered a completely new world. First of all, I met friendly people in the teaching staff. The first shock was my Polish teacher, an inestimable professor Piontkowski, who managed to inculcate an idea of love towards our mother tongue into us. He didn't care how I wrote. He cared what I wrote. Of course, he took up a heroic fight against my dyslexia. His method was scribing. It lied in my obligatory rewriting 7 pages a week from a free to choose book in a special notebook. In a magic way, that mechanical copying letters liberated me from fear of writing.

Thanks to that man, my handwriting can be read today with no need of using any special equipment. Also, he noticed a talent for writing in me. He infected me with a passion for telling stories. Most of my papers received the highest grades. He had taught me to write what I felt and thought. When I wrote anything that was not in accordance with the doctrine, he always asked me to defend my arguments in front of the class. When I did that in a convincing way, I got the highest marks, but when it seemed that I was writing nonsense, I got the lowest. As well, he supported my love for theatre. Thanks to that, my time in high school was divided among the rehearsals in the "Lucky Thirteen" cabaret, school lessons and scouts' meetings. Basically, already then I didn't have time for private life.

Another person in school, who shared my passions, was our female tutor. Mrs. Pleskacz, who appeared in the school together with us, went down in my private history of memory because of two facts. The first was her pregnancy. For the first year of our studying, we were observing with joy her growing belly and her constantly concerned face.

The other fact was our shared passion for ancient history. When she discovered, that I loved antiquity, our lessons became a theatre. I was teaching most of the lessons that year. I was telling the class about wonders of the ancient world. Professor Pleskacz used to complement my colorful stories with historical dates, for which I never had head. Today I smile recalling the moments, when I used to come to her after the lesson finished and asked what I should prepare for the next lesson.

I had been never elected for the class's student council, but I was the only person, who was capable of arranging everything. I used to hang around in the teachers' common room; I was on good terms with the principals. I had been accepted. When we went away for so called "green school" trip, my relations with the woman tutor still tightened up. Girls and boys from my class felt like making small parties, which were not officially allowed. It's obvious, that drinking alcohol at school trips is forbidden for the high school youth. Though, our company found a solution. As a scouts' instructor I couldn't drink alcohol at all. At least, officially or I could loose my position. That's why I wasn't taken into consideration as an organizer of class benders during trips. However, I was perfect for the rear area protection. Thus, when I knew that a party was going to begin, I used to go to the tutor's room and proposed that we go for a walk. Usually, we used to go to one of the highlander cafes. Thanks to those escapades, I learned to appreciate the taste of good coffee and I got to know many interesting stories from the private lives of our teachers.

Apart from our female tutor and a teacher of Polish language, teacher of mathematics my friends at high school were teachers. Professor Kusak was a regular eccentric. An enthusiast of tourism, the head of the school circle of the PTTK (Polish Tourist Country-Lovers' Association), he knew intuitively I was his kindred spirit. I owe him, that I concluded my education in that school favorably. At the first class he oriented himself, that mathematics was a subject as strange to me as ballet to a body-builder.

I promised him to take part in all the trips and camps that he organized. In return for that, he had never checked my school-tests. I was always getting a satisfactory grade. I still remember, when he told me just before the High School Diploma examinations: "*Don't you even think about choosing mathematics at the exams, God forbid for I won't be able to protect you there.*"

We went through much with professor Kusak. At one of the walking tours, I contracted a scar on my chin, which I have to this day. The cause was quite simple. I wanted to shave myself. And before the tour, I got a gift from my grandma, an archaic electric shaver that my grandfather used to use. But the shaver shaved not only my facial hair, but also a bit of the skin from my chin.

During my high school education, I was maintaining contact with father. It became a tradition to meet every month at a family dinner at a restaurant, at which I was invited.

Usually, I met there my father, his partner, her sister and her child. Because my father was a famous in Poland gynecologist society, soon I became known among girls, as the one, who could help them in "those" matters. I became a confidant and an adviser of most of the girls in my class. It came to ridiculous situations, when I was accosted at school breaks and asked about various gynecological problems. The truth was that my dad had always received my friends for free. One day I couldn't stand it and when one of them asked me about her problem, I answered: "*I cannot infer from a tale, I would have to see it.*" Imagine that that girl was convinced that if I saw "the problem," I would know what the matter was.

In high school also was still working in a cabaret. And I was still dating Iwona. She was the first woman I slept with. We were planning to get married. Though, I still couldn't find in her something that I was looking for. After a tough period, we split. A few years later I attended her wedding. I hope she has shaped her life conveniently.

The second woman in my life was Basia. She was my aide in the theatrical scouting troop, which we had created and used to run together. Our relationship didn't last long, it was very stormy.

She was trying to find her ex-boyfriend in me. I was trying to find in her something, which I was desperately looking for in every woman. We both hadn't found what we were looking for. The effect was an intoxicating night spent at one of the camps and equally dramatic my leaving the scouting organization. The cup of bitterness was filled up because of the changes in this organization that I already mentioned before.

For the four years of high school, the closest person to me had been Marzena. That young, possessed with the spirit of a modern girl, was the best friend to me. I was her confidant. She used to come to me with every problem. In secret, I loved her passionately, knowing that she was out of my reach. She was my never fulfilled love.

I will never forget, when in 3 class she came to me weeping after they had broken off with a very handsome man. She said: *"Szymon, there are no more men in this world."* Then I said, *"And what about me?"* "You are not a man," I heard. I stopped being angry at her half a year later.

At high school, I took possession of the school theatre. All the ceremonies, festivities, and school events were directed by me. I still remember those meetings in the principal's office, when we were deliberating, what was going to be presented at the next session of celebration. Also then, I met one of the managers of the Powszechny Theatre in Warsaw. Thanks to him, my adventure with a dramatic theatre began. That was a full professional theatre and in comparison with that my roles in the Ochota Theatre, in the "Lucky Thirteen" and other formations faded into insignificance.

Ryszard Jakubisiak was a colorful individual. He had a charisma and he knew how to infect people with his passion. He was the one who created an amateur theatre Parabuch, in which I started my adventure with drama. At the beginning, we were performing in a hall rented on the Warsaw Old Town. With time, I managed to convince the two school principals to give a shelter to Parabuch in our school stage. It was on the Parabuch stage, where I challenged a monstrous role in the "Greek Envoys" and I got to the stage of the Powszechny Theater. Also, I must admit, that Parabuch changed my life in a way I would never suspect it might change. It helped me to discover, who I really was.

It was in Parabuch I met my last girlfriend. I called her Margot. She was younger than me, she was trusting and we fell in passionate love together. Basically, I met her not at the Parabuch, but in its youth section, that was called Paradox. One of our performances went down in history. While parodying a Skoluba's Aria from Moniuszko's opera "The Haunted Manor," we were making fun of our two female principals. How extraordinary, we had never had any problems for that reason. In Parabuch I used to act mainly in comedies. We loved classic works, which resulted in my first award for the leading male role, I won this at the overview of theatre formations in Zielonka. I sill remember some of he lines of the Master from A. Fredro's comedy "A Candle Has Faded," which brought me that victory.

As well, for me high school was the time of my adolescence and discovering the truth about myself. In the last class I was dating Margot, and at the same time I was beginning to be interested in boys. But I was trying to make myself believe that that was a temporary fascination, harmless fabrications, which would fade away with time. I continued to think so for quite a long time, in spite of myself and everybody else. Many years later, Marzena told me, that everyone in our class knew I was gay, but nobody made any fuss about it. What a pity I didn't know it. Then, I wouldn't have hurt Margot.

Though before I learned this fact about me something happened which determined my decision about becoming independent. Once, when we were playing in my room naked, unexpectedly, Adam came back home. He entered my room without knocking at the door, as it was in his habit. He froze in the doorway and only on my explicit demand, he retreated. Later, mum told me, that he made a row, because as he said, he didn't want to have a brothel at home.

I didn't have good relations with Adam during my high school. He was attached to home and its surroundings very much. Working in the garden, chopping wood for fuel, and caring for bees and doves was most important to him. While I was free as a bird of the air. I had been already working as an extra in the Powszechny Theatre. It often happened that I was coming home after midnight. Arguments came about; the atmosphere was becoming more and more heavy. In the meantime I was finishing high school.

For the final exams subjects I chose Polish language, which was obligatory, and biology. If you got a good grade from Polish at the end of the year and you got a good grade at high school finals, you could count on an exemption from the oral exam. I remember from the finals exams I was sitting in one of the last rows and I was writing a composition on the role of war in the literature. Teachers were walking to and from the room. One moment, our female tutor came to a halt next to me and with her eyes fixed upon the far end of the classroom, she asked me in theatrical whisper: "*Do you know anything on the 1?*" "*But I'm writing on the third one, professor,*" I answered. "*But Aśka is writing on the first one and she doesn't quite cope with it.*" "*What should I do?*" I asked slightly surprised. Write down what you know on a sheet of paper. I did so. I quickly wrote a dozen or so points related to the first topic. I called the tutor to come to me under the pretence of asking for a sandwich. The tutor came, leaned over me and with her eyes fixed upon the distance, she grabbed the sheet of paper under the tray with sandwiches. In the same way she supplied Aśka with the sheet of paper. I thought that I would burst with laughter.

Another funny story connected with the high school finals was my written exam in biology. I drew a topic "Structure and function of a leaf at seminal plants." I knew that according to the program, I should have written four foolscap pages minimum. Guess, how much can you write about a leaf? So I started with evolution and I didn't even noticed when I gathered speed and had written 14 pages. When I had given my paper back and left the classroom, a chemistry woman teacher dashed out of the room and commented in full voice: "*Niemiec, for God's sake! Have you created an epic, who is going to check this?!!*"

It turned out that I got 5 from Polish and I got 4 from biology, because I hadn't described a structure of a stem. Hmmmm, you'll never know what the people giving grades would want.

I was planning, that after graduating high school, I would try to apply to the State College of Theatrical Arts. Though, knowing that there were 20 people on one place, at the same time I applied for Balkan Department at the Warsaw University. They didn't admit me at the theatrical college, though I had a diploma of theatrical instructor. But I didn't go for the University, as well. In the meantime, my father, who managed to reconcile himself to the fact that he wouldn't make a medical doctor of me, pushed me into the embrace of the College of Communication and Social Media in Warsaw. Literally, he pushed me, because he committed himself to paying the tuition. As it turned out later, it was just the right move.

After an interview I was admitted at the first year of political science. Then, my journalistic career began.

Going over to the other side...

For me, the period of college was also a period of rapid changes. First of all, I moved to a different place. After another row with Adam, we came into the conclusion with mum that the situation couldn't last any longer. Before my mum left for holidays and cause she didn't want to leave me alone, she sent me to father. While I had been living with him for a few months, I started to observe changes in me.

First of all, having an access the computer, I started to get to know the world of the Internet. I already had my own PC assembled, equipped with a phone modem, so the telephone bills grew bigger and bigger. There were no Internet Cafés, never mind, there were no chats based in Java. The Internet was in the phase of developing.

My first acquaintances I made by means of KAMchat that was a conversation room based on pure HTML and a prototype of an Internet communicator that was a special program used for chat released by Microsoft. Using that communicator I found a channel #polskagay. As I've already mentioned, I was attracted to men already before, but it didn't go beyond the sphere of fantasy. Internet chat together with one of the first Polish gay channels convinced me to overcome the magic barrier between fantasy and the real world. I was then a crazy 17-year-old boy furnished with a great trust in people, which I hadn't got rid of till today. One day, when I was talking to gays from all over Poland on the Internet, someone asked me for a private conversation. It turned out, that he was Warsaw, just like me. We were talking for a few hours and then he suggested a meeting in real. Usually, I used to refuse in similar situations, and the conversations used to end at that point. But this time it was to be different. Guided by an instinct, I agreed to meet. We made an appointment near my father's flat, at a bus stop. I came one hour earlier, as I was in a habit of arriving earlier. It was a beautiful September afternoon. Suddenly, I saw Him. He was older than me; he had beautiful, long fair hair and a nicely shaped body. He came up to me and started to talk. We decided to go for a walk to the Kampinos Forest.

I don't remember much from the walk, but I know that it ended at my home. We both felt like having sex. He, as the experienced one, desired me. I was in a panic and I started to wonder, if I really wanted that. The lights went off, there was silence, and darkness fell.

The first touch... the first kiss... I didn't even notice when we both were naked. The rest went very fast, too fast. For him, I was just another man he slept with. They say you never forget your first time. There must be something in it, though over 10 years have passed, I still remember the scent of his hair and the taste of his skin. We had met never again. He went away his way and I flung into the college, theatre and new and fascinating discoveries. At those times, I was still sure, I was simply a bisexual. I continued to date Margot, who had never learned about my cheating on her. If this book ever gets into her hands, she will have absolute right to call me a perfect bastard. And she will be right.

We split up with Margot at my first year of college. At that time, I already knew that I was attracted to men practically exclusively and that I wasn't able to find in a woman that something that I was really looking for. The parting was very painful for both of us. She had suffered for very many months, and once when I happened to meet her a few years later, I saw the same reproach in her eyes.

I suspect that her love for me was effectively replaced with hatred. She was one of the first persons, who got to know that I was attracted to men. She didn't want to believe it until one day, when we were walking the street and we looked back at the same hunk. In spite of tears in her eyes, we both burst in laughter. Probably, she believed me then.

After the academic year had started, I moved to my grandma's flat. We sold the splendid villa in Sadyba and we bought two flats; one at Powsińska Street the other one at Korczyńska Street. We rented the smaller one, with two rooms, to one of mum's acquaintances from Canada. Grandma moved to the bigger one.

Because the atmosphere at my mum's home was close to exploding, we though that the best would be if I moved to live with grandma. An additional advantage was a perfect bus connection with my college on Bielany.

The college was a period of transforming, maturing and reconciling with me. Still I was hiding the truth about me from most of the people. Basically, until the last year of college, nobody knew I was gay. I was picking up girls, dating; I served as a confidant and a confessor for all the girls from the year. And at the same time, I was secretly dating various guys, who were interested solely in my body. I'm not writing this to boast. Though, I believe that all the people who considered me, and still consider, being an ideal, deserving to know the truth. I'm not an ideal nor had I never been the one.

The first vocation...

At the first year of college, I also started to work. Thanks to my mentor, an editor Wojciech Giełżyński, who was also the president of the college, ten freshmen volunteers got to work with the editorial staff of a daily Życie Warszawy for student training. That was a day before Fat Thursday. In the first place, we were invited to an office by the then editor-in-chief of the newspaper, Aleksander Ćwiećko, who after a few introductory words, asked us to go to the City Department and look around to find anything to do there. Immediately, the manager of the Department sent us to the city with a command to acquire maximum information on the feast falling on the following day. We were to visit most of the Warsaw cake shops and to learn about donuts as much as one could. Later, we were to get back to the editorial office and describe everything that we saw. Out of 10 volunteers, 4 had got back to the editorial office. The rest decided that they didn't like it. We shared our findings and wrote a text, which after countless editorial corrections was published the following day with our initials. That was my first press publication.

I remember that the next day the editor-in-chief called four of us to his office, and handed out a small red book entitled "Press Law." He asked us to come to him the following day to discuss it. That was a wonderful experience to see an expert journalist, who decided to devote his time to show us, greenhorn students the basic rules of the journalist profession. I leaned much from him.

With time, when I became a reporter of the City Department, I started to write about everything that was going on in the city. In the meantime, a part of our editorial team has left together with Tomasz Wołek to create a new daily. We treated them as traitors. And we, the students of the College of Communication and Social Media, were offered a chance to publish our own supplement titled "Students' Life." It was a weekly supplement to the newspaper that we were to create totally independently for the tribe of students. I became a managing editor of the department and with time, the editor-in-chief. Thanks to that, during half a year of publishing the supplement, I learned not only a solid journalist's craft, but also the rules of making up columns and pages, knowledge of graphic computer programs, and all what a reader cannot see when he grasps a finished newspaper. It seemed to me that a run of good luck would last for ever.

Unfortunately, they changed the editor-in-chief of the newspaper. A new man, whose second name I don't even remember, incited by the students of the journalist department of the Warsaw University, he decided to change the personnel of the editorial staff of the supplement. There would be nothing wrong with it; if not the manner he did it.

One December day, we were torn away from working on the Christmas issue and asked to come to the chief's office. He informed us that he wasn't satisfied with the supplement and he was offered a proposal from the journalist department of the WU, which wanted to take over the supplement. But the decision was going to be taken the following day, after they evaluated the issue. It was surprising insomuch, that our pages had never been evaluated at the meeting of the editorial council. The number of favorable opinions that we got from other departments and in the letters from the readers, gave us a deceptive hope, that we were doing a good job. That's why we went for the evaluation in a good mood. The editorial office was to evaluate every page of the issue very precisely. There was a tradition that evaluation was made by one department. The issue, in which our supplement was published, was to be evaluated by the Culture Department, which editors were deadly afraid of losing their positions. They were usually very meticulous in their evaluations. The meeting was getting drawn out and we were waiting impatiently for our turn. Our supplement numbered two pages. When the evaluating editor turned the page and got to our spread, we heard: *"And now, the student supplement, my favorite. As usual crappy. So, let's go further on."* We froze. We expected a critique, some content-related or at least technical objections but not this horrible unsubstantiated declaration.

After the meeting I approached the editor-in-chief and asked him outright: "Mr. Editor, does it mean that you remove us?" "Yes," he said in passing. "Can we at least say goodbye to our readers?" "Feel free to do it," he replied without a glance in my direction.

"When you are leaving, let it be a notorious leaving," editor Giełżyński used to say. So, we decided to let everyone know about our leaving. We prepared two columns, as usual with a little difference. More than a half of the first page was taken by a huge obituary notice with a headline: "The late Students' Life." Below, in a very personal article, I described the whole story of the supplement and its shutting down. I was afraid that I might exaggerate, so I sent the text for a review to editor Giełżyński. After fifteen minutes I got a phone call: *"We take it. It's great text. Let it sting them quickly."*

Of course we all are equal, but I have a key!

The supplement went through proof reading, making up columns and was accepted by the managing editor of the editorial office. Unfortunately, colleagues from the Culture Department had spotted it and they alarmed the chief. The latest one burst into the editorial office yelling at the managing editor, that he was to remove the text immediately and at me to get out and that he placed a ban on my entering the building until he was no longer the editor-in-chief.

I didn't bother too much about that, for I knew that I had the president of my college and many journalists on my side and I left with credit. You can imagine my surprise, when two days later my text appeared in an everyday issue of the newspaper amended with an insulting commentary by the editor-in-chief. Of, course I knew that nobody would even notice my correction, but it was the president of the college who got involved in the issue. His long and very sharp in tone letter was published in a correction mode the following day. The editor-in-chief of the ŻW had the devil to pay, while I was walking through the corridors of the college in the glory and splendor of the first student repressed for the freedom of speech.

I came back onto the columns of that newspaper already as a main character of articles and overages a few years later. Right now, when I'm writing these words, the daily newspaper, in which I was winning my journalist epaulettes, has gone to the dogs completely. It's licking the right-wing fanatics' boots outdoing the WPROST weekly in vilifying the moral authorities of this world. I can admit proudly, that as once I was gated by the newspaper, now the newspaper is gated by me and I will never publish any of their statements. Let's call it a little, petty revenge after years. Those times, I, feeling disappointed with a sudden loss of possibility of describing students' life, together with friends from the year, established our own students' paper. We called it "Leser." I registered the title in the court and I felt like a real publisher, though the first issues were printed on the college Xerox machine. The "Leser" had quite a big readership and it would have probably last longer if not my eternal impatience and constantly new ideas coming to my head.

After I left Życie Warszawy, I was still getting practical training in a weekend supplement to Super Ekspress daily newspaper. My training coincided in time with a huge flood in the south of Poland. I remember, when one day, feeling bored in the editorial office, an Internet forum caught my eye, where one of the discussion topics concerned Wrocław, which was flooded then.

The main author was a boy describing what online he was seeing currently. All of us were seconding him with bated breath the more intensively, cause his every few minutes more and more dramatic entries appeared. Finally, the situation was that the whole editorial staff and most of the news department were sitting in front of my computer screen. Everyone was waiting for the next note.

The last one sounded: "*I have to stop. The power has been cut off for several minutes, my cell will die in a minute and UPS is also dying. Water reaches up to my ankles. I can see an amphibious vehicle. Cross your fingers.*"

The man lived on the third floor in a district of block of flats. His whole block of flats had been evacuated few hours before, and he was the only person who had hidden and stayed there to inform other people, what was happening. When they cut him off the telephone, he connected to his mobile and he reported through that. In those times, that kind of service wasn't offered by any of the telecommunication operators, so he was connecting via a TPSA 's number, open to general use. I still have no idea, how he connected his mobile to the computer at the times, when the cables and tools which are indispensable for that were not available, as today. But being a computer science student, he must have helped it in some way. The whole of Poland was rooting for him.

As far as I know, he was saved, but I can't forget the day, when the editorial staff were sitting in front of the computer screen and praying for him to write anything. A story about internauts during the flood arose of that.

Within the breaks between work in successive editorial offices and classes at college, I was leading quite a normal life. I was living with grandma. I was spending much time on the Internet and writing new texts.

I owed my quite accidental contacts with men to the Internet, though in those times there was only one Polish site devoted to gays and nobody even heard about gay chats.

My mum engaged in a work with her two familiar psychologists, who decided to create the first in Poland organization training youth leaders. The Public Youth Academy was a very ambitious project. In that new, just arising reality, it was extremely difficult to create a framework of democracy. But Jacek and Dorota Jakubowski had accurately sensed that you had to educate youth in the first place. Young people infected with the ideas of democracy were the perfect future leaders, available to build common good. I plunged into their project and I was helping them as much as I could. With time, when our Canadian friends left our second flat, the office of PYA moved into there. My mum persuaded the Jakubowkis to let me live in one of their two rooms. That gave me nearly total independence and they acquired a familiar full time worker for their office.

When I started to live independently, I got more possibilities to open to the world. One day, when I was spending my time on the gay site that I've already mentioned, a boy started a conversation with me. He asked me if knew that a new way of Internet communication was coming into being and a few people created a special channel for the Polish gays. In this way I discovered IRC.

When I downloaded IRC program for the first time, and I entered the #gaypl site, there were 6 people there. Soon, that group was to become my second family. Today, when on the Polish Internet there are a few hundred gay chats, and the most popular of them is visited by a few thousand people every day, that six person group communicating with each other thanks to a complicated set of commands and marks seem funny today.

I remember my first blunder. It was about my nick, my Internet alias. Before that I was using nick "shaman" everywhere on the net. The nick came from my interest in parapsychology and a total contestation of the Roman Church. When I entered the IRC, I was trying to log under the same nick unconsciously. Though, it turned out, that it had already been taken by someone else. Some time had to pass before I met a young admirer of Greek on the net, who invented the nick for me that I've been using to this day; Technites. It means a craftsman, a Master and a Teacher at the same time. I liked it and it stuck to me for ever.

For me, entering the IRC world meant not only making new acquaintances it also meant entering the gay world. A gay, who lives in Warsaw today, has a choice of 13 clubs, including two with dancing halls, two resilient gay organizations and a dozen or so Internet sites. I used to have a choice of 4 clubs, one Internet site and one gay organization. Finally, one day I decided to summon up enough courage and go to a club. I made an appointment with friends from IRC and we went to the club at Koźla Street. At present, when you mention the Goats, few people know what that was. But at those times, it was a cultic spot. That microscopic clubhouse located in a basement of an apartment house on the New Town used to attract crowds of people every night. Despite of the popular opinion, the biggest crowds collected there on Wednesdays.

To help you imagine the Goats, I suggest making a following experiment: Imagine a can of sardines. Take out the sardines. Grab another can of sardines, and again, take out the sardines.

Mix the sardines with confetti, pour some beer and keep that in the cigarette smoke for some time. Then, push that into one can. Close the can. Make a little hole in the bottom. Put the can over a candle. Light the whole thing up with a stroboscope. And peer inside the can through the little opening. You will see the Goats on Wednesdays.

You may wonder why that poky, dirty and not quite interesting place attracted those crowds. It is not easy to answer the question. Or maybe it is not possible at all. I think that each of us was attracted by a different thing. I for example was attracted there by an illusory feeling of safety and the atmosphere. That illusory feeling of safety came from the fact, that the club's door was always closed. There was a doorbell. And a broad-shouldered bodyguard standing in the doorway opened the door exclusively to the people he knew by sight or to those, who were recommended by frequent visitors. Then, we thought it was the triumph of dreams, because we were simply ourselves there. You didn't have to afraid that you meet a person from your work, school or a family member. Some of the frequent visitors still used to be haunted by recollection of an infamous operation Hyacinth. In the emerging new democracy, simply nobody discussed a topic of homosexuality. The times of gays' great coming out into the open were still ahead of us and everyone cared for protecting their privacy.

Though, on the other hand, the situation wasn't that tragic. At the Goats, groups of mutual support, and sometimes of adoration, were arising. We, people from IRC used to be a powerful team. We even used to have our own sofa, which was dirty and spotted, and stood in a corner of the tiny room. That sofa made up our empire. That was the sofa I landed on, when I entered the gay club for the first time.

It was still early and the club was quite empty. Usually, the climax of the number of people fell on 23:00, so at 20:00, when I came into the club, it was quite deserted.

I was sitting on the sofa in a company of AQQ and Maciejka - two prepossessing, older than me, and I was absorbing the atmosphere of the "forbidden fruit" with every pore of my skin. When the club began to be crowded, a procession appeared on the stairs. The first one was going a well-built fair-haired man with an eternally smiling face. Two young and slim boys with their eyes fixed on him followed. The whole three of them were going down the stairs and greeting everyone one by one. They looked very majestically. They turned their steps toward us and the greeting started. The blond man shook my hand and introduced himself as Pacco. It took my breath away. Pacco was one of the first founders of gays' IRC in Poland. Many regarded him as a god of the Internet. I managed only to spit out: *"So, you are THAT Pacco?"* He looked at me with his blue, eternally amused eyes and asked: *"And who are you?"* "Shaman," I answered quietly. *"Oh… nice to meet you,"* he said and his entourage followed. At that moment I couldn't have known, that fate would make our ways intersect for quite a long time.

The times had their specific rituals. One of them was a ritual of signing a list. You may say that these were the beginnings of the Warsaw gay clubbing. Every Wednesday, around 20:00, the whole society gathered in the Goats. Usually, gathering of people more or less to 23:00, when the crowd in the club was reaching its peak and you couldn't stand inside. Then, usually a parole was said: "OK, the list has been signed."

For most of us, that was a signal to march out. We were redeploying in smaller and bigger groups into the direction of the Babka roundabout, where the second Warsaw gay club was located. Mykonos was a splendid imitation of a Greek tavern which walls were decorated with ancient erotic graphics. It attracted everyone. We used to get there around midnight and stayed there till morning. At least, it used to happen so up to the moment when the second gay disco club, called Paradise was opened on the territory of the Skra Stadium. It was the second, for the first one was Rudawka located in the Praga district. Though, Rudawka was soon shut down and we were left with Paradise with its huge, glassed dancing hall and a smaller bar room. We used to drink a few beers in the Mykonos, appear in the Paradise around 4 in the morning and stay on the dancing floor up till the morning light and a DJ, who finished playing, expelled us into the outside. That ritual used to repeat every week. If anyone of our regular group couldn't appear in any of the spots, the most often at least a dozen or so e-mails or calls with questions of the kind "Are you alive? Are you OK? What happened to you?" were awaiting him.

Another little ritual related to the Paradise was the way DJ Beki was beginning to finish to play. That man has gone down in history thanks to his unconventional attitude towards life. For example, during the whole party he used to wear his legendary fur slippers and sunglasses hiding half of his face. When the party was coming to an end, and Beki wasn't going to prolong it, he always used to play one song. When we heard "Wsiąść do pociągu byle jakiego" from the loudspeakers, we all knew that there was no hope for us. That was always the last song. Beki had never let anyone convince him. After that piece, he simply used to turn off the music and switch off the lights.

When Beki died of AIDS, as one of the first official casualties in our society, with him a certain piece of us died, as well. The next DJs in the Paradise weren't so close to us, as he used to be.

Development of the club life in no way collided with the development of the virtual world. Besides, in a way, those two worlds used to complement one another. At an IRC channel, where I could be found very often, I met again Pacco, who then lived together with McCozy, whom he used to call his "child." The two had never been a couple, but there existed a specific Master-Disciple relation between them. Then McCozy's partner was Anvero. That was the two boys, whom I saw accompanying Pacco on my first visit at the Goats.

One sunny day, as usual I entered IRC and I was sitting and talking to a new person. The channel was at its peak of popularity, and we, the administrators, were happy as a clam, when a number of users registered on the channel were exceeding the next magic tens. Already then, some public spirit instincts were awakening in me, for basically I was the only one who took responsibility for the new users.

During one of such "object-lessons," Pacco appeared on the channel and asked if anyone felt like going with him for a walk. I volunteered and we made an appointment at the Plac Na Rozdrożu, at the place, where we both had a good bus connection. In those times Pacco lived in the Praga district.

At that moment I didn't sense, that another great change was drawing close in my live. I was waiting for him a few minutes. When he approached me, he introduced himself, as if we had never met before. Since that moment, I knew his first name was Adam. For the first time, he surprised me during the first five minutes of conversation, when he said: "*I hope that also for you it's only a walk, not an offer of sex. I don't go to bed with friends.*" I choked for two reasons. Firstly, because I didn't care for sex with him at all and secondly, he admitted me to the circle of his friends.

That afternoon we were walking through the whole Łazienki park and having fun. Also, on that occasion we began overfeeding ducks in the park. It consisted in buying a substantial loaf of bread and feeding one, chosen duck until it popped. It had never come to popping of a duck, probably because we ran short of bread. As you see, I've never quite liked those feathered monsters.

Later, we shared the story about over feeding the ducks with other IRC users. And Adam started to be a regular visitor at my home, and together with him, also his friends, our common acquaintances from IRC and people whom we met in the clubs. At some moment, my modest flat became an open house and such it has remained up to the present.

Pacco became my very close friend. With time he moved out from his "children" and he moved back to his parents again. He visited me quite often; sometimes he even stayed for the night. Time was passing by slowly alternating visiting clubs, with writing for consecutive papers and looking for love. The year 1977 was approaching.

A Rainbow Hued Bird in a Golden Cage.

Life of gays in Warsaw of those times was mainly in the clubs. Media remained silent about us; nobody raised the question of homosexuality in public. We used to live in closed ghettos, isolated from the external world with bodyguards in clubs and with curtained windows. We didn't realize that life could be different. Also, not many of us were fighters ready to start the struggle. We were only reading magazines published for us, we were spending time on the Internet and we were romping in the clubs.

The social life was flourishing. Since the beginning of high school, my family life was divided between two homes. At least once a month, my father used to invite me to a restaurant or to his villa in Lipki Stare. There, I used to spend time with him, his partner Magda, her sister and her niece. The ritual of those meetings had lasted unchanged for years. It sometimes bore fruit of interesting experience. It was Magda, who uncovered the secrets of the French cuisine for me. And thanks to a visit with my father to one of the first in Warsaw Japanese restaurants, I fell in love with sushi. My first contact with that Japanese treat is still on my memory, also for its connection with religious and theatrical sphere.

**If you are looking for way out,
train station is this way...**

At that time, I used to cooperate with a young and talented stage-manager Grzegorz Reszko from the Ochota theatre. Together with friends we were staging Paul Bartz's play "Dinner Played Four Hands." It's a wonderful story about a fictional dinner of Friderick Handel and Johann Sebastian Bach. I took part in that performance as operating personnel. I attended to the sound. One of the last performances was held in the basement of the church at the Plac Zbawiciela in Warsaw. There is a final scene in the drama, in which the main role plays one of the most popular music pieces by Handel. According to the scenario, Hallelujah from "Messiah" was to be played on the highest level of the sound volume. Though, I didn't suspect that the acoustics in the basement of the church was so great. The impression was electrifying, but it was nothing in comparison what happened after the performance.

When the viewers had already left, and we were packing up our equipment, we spotted a priest walking in our direction staggering with laughter. He stopped in front of us and while doing his best to keep serious, asked us if we realized that we worked a miracle.

Our surprised faces encouraged him to make explanation. It appeared that he was sitting in the upper church in a confessional, when a weeping woman came to him informing that she had just experienced a revelation. She was sobbing and telling the priest that she hadn't gone to church for years, but her mother died and she came there to settle the matters related to arranging the funeral. "I'm entering the main nave of the church," she said. "And suddenly, from all the directions, from the ground, from heaven and from all the sides, I can hear angelic choir. Dear father that was a miracle!"

It turned out, that the basement of the church was connected to the upper church with a network of numerous ventilating ducts. Our music drifted through those channels causing an effect of a spatial sound. A person standing in the middle of the main nave actually could have an impression that the sound reached her from all the directions simultaneously. I don't know if I should feel proud because of that forced conversion, but I remember that we were very amused.

After the performance I met my father, who invited me to a Japanese restaurant for sushi. If I may give advice to a beginning gourmet, I suggest never eating too much for the first time. I got a really substantial helpful, and because I hadn't known yet the right proportion of soy sauce and horseradish, in which you dip pieces of fish, I seriously exaggerated. I felt sick all day.

Apart from that little boob, I still have very pleasant memories from those culinary meetings with my father and Magda. Also, I had gone with Magda and her sister for a Buddhist camp, where I got to know the wonderful spirituality of yoga. Also there, I came across Christian meditations in the Franciscan order. Elements of those two traditions underline my attitude towards life.

Transition from a closet to the Polish Bitches' Club.

Everything started to go wrong at the moment, when, encouraged by friends, I changed color of my hair. It wasn't a radical change, by no means. I added a ginger shine to my natural brown color. At the next meeting with father, Magda stated that it suited me, and father commented that it was solely my business. All hell broke loose the next day. It turned out, that father called mum and he shouted out into the receiver, that she brought up his son to be a gay. He was threatening with breaking contact and said that he wanted me to change the surname not to allow me to defame his clan. That was a moment when my mum decided on a serious talk with me. It was a terrible moment for both of us.

It was an afternoon. We were sitting leaning over mugs of coffee and remaining silent. It was obvious, that something was eating her, but I was waiting for her move. Then, mum looked at me and with a heavy heart she asked me if I was a homosexual.

I had my heart in my mouth. Of course, I could have lied, denied and pretended. But I knew that there was no point in that. Sooner or later, the thing must come to light.

I looked into her eyes and confessed. I saw the shine in her eyes fading away. Then, there was another moment of silence and finally the most important and most beautiful words I could hear were uttered. "*You know that it will be difficult for me to live with this*," she said. "*But you are my son and I will never stop loving you.*" Then, she said she had to come back home. The next two weeks were a nightmare for me. I was calling her at least twice a day to make sure if she was all right. I always heard the same, sad voice assuring me that everything was all right.

Not before a few years later, I got to know that my mum spend those two weeks sitting at home and drinking one drink after another and trying to collect herself. She had to reconcile herself to the truth, which after all she had already known before. Basically, that question she asked me was her last hope, that maybe she had been wrong.

As she stated later in the interviews, she became suspicious when I was 16. But she was really lucky, for she met a couple of excellent and experienced psychologists in persons of Jacek and Dorota. Both of them were preparing her for that moment. They were explaining what homosexuality was and how she could help me. I am and always will be grateful to them for that. They have saved not only her, but also me. Thanks to them, the next years, I and my mum were learning how to live. She learned how to be a mother of a gay. And me how to be a son of the mother, who knew about her son that he was gay.

Thanks to cooperation with the Jakubowskis, my mum found strength in herself to tell about me to the grandmas, to her partner and to help other parents, whom I started to send to her a few years later.

Soon, second cousins were to learn about me. Meanwhile, in the Paradise, a generation change was happening. More and more young people were appearing. They were obsessed with sex, having fun and heavy drinking. Drugs were beginning to conquer the market and fortunately for us, they were not popular in gay clubs. Whereas alcohol, yes, of course.

Looking back at those events from the prospect of 10 years, I may say that we constituted a substitute of a family for one another. We used to stick together, everyone knew everyone, and usually every newcomer was welcomed with distrust.

Of course, in that kind of society, it was difficult to keep secret one's private life, so information who slept with whom and in what configuration, constituted a public secret. Though, everything was treated with tongue in cheek. When more youth was coming to the Paradise club, also less pleasant situations started to happen. Drunken teenagers, who appeared more and more frequently, couldn't behave adequately in a situation. They were becoming suspicious, that everybody slept with everybody, and that in turn raised jealousy and aggression. Of course, fighting with that kind of insults with help of reasonable and matter-of-fact arguments had never brought any good results. So we decided to fight it with a weapon that we were using perfectly well. That was sarcasm and satire. In this way, a Club of Polish Bitches was born.

It was an elitist group created by us for a laugh. We had our code of conduct and rules that we obeyed strictly. Of course, that had nothing in common with prostitution or sex for money. Sex became a taboo sphere, secured strictly with the rules of the code. I know, it may be difficult to understand, but after a few months we were convulsed with laughter watching subsequent teenagers coming up to our table and asking if they could buy us a beer. Most often, we agreed, for who wouldn't have taken an opportunity? Usually, after the first round, a time-honored question was uttered, if they had a chance to get to our elitist club. An insult "you, bitch" disappeared from the Paradise, cause suddenly it was no longer an insult, but a synonym of the elitist. It had lasted for quite a long time, until we felt bored with that game and the club died of natural causes.

Meanwhile, IRC was at its peak of development. It happened that at the #gaypl channel, 600 persons appeared at the same time. There were arising local and specialist channels. Those of us, who were here from the very beginning, were taking care of controlling and moderating discussions. We were operating bots, i.e. small programs administrating the channel, we were teaching the newcomers our Internet etiquette and we were acting as advisers in difficult moments. Pacco organized the first reunion in Łódź. I didn't go there. Though, I remember a funny story connected with that event. When a train from Warsaw rolled onto the platform, a delegation of IRC users from Łódź was waiting at the station. When they saw Pacco getting off the train and carrying quite a big suitcase, someone observed: *"Look, Pacco has come with his vanity bag."* Adam glanced at the company kind-heartedly and said: *"No, these are only my clothes. McCozy is carrying the vanity bag."* At that moment, just behind his back, a mentioned IRC user appeared loaded with two huge suitcases. At first, the company froze, and then they burst out laughing. I'll only add that it was a two-day reunion.

The year 1997 was slowly coming to end, and my contacts with Ula and Pacco were becoming closer and closer. Christmas was coming near. And because everyone was leaving for their families, we decided to meet one day before and share presents. It was the time, when Pacco was visiting me practically every day. Sometimes he was waiting for me under the door, when I was coming back from the editorial office. That's why I hit upon an idea to give him a special Christmas gift.

When Adam unpacked a box, which I gave him, he found there a set of keys to my flat and a note: "Think, if you would entrust the key to your home to your best friend. If not, change your friends." The atmosphere was moving, warm and pleasant. None of us had predicted how prophetic that gift would appear soon. The next day was Christmas Vigil. We parted, everyone joined their families. Ula left for her cousins in Hajnówka, I went to my mum near Warsaw, and Pacco went to his parents living in the center of Warsaw.

We were sitting at a table at my mum's home together with grandma Wandzia, grandma Walerka, Adam's mother. Suddenly a phone rang. Mum picks it up and said it was for me. In the receiver I heard Pacco's very sad voice, who informed me that his parents have just turned him onto the street. He told me, that he was preparing Christmas Vigil dinner all day. He was cooking up, cleaning and generally preparing house, while the rest of his family was sitting in armchairs and drinking beer after beer. When everything was ready, his father in a drunken vision started to shout out that he was not going to sit at the Christmas table with

a gay. And then, he slapped him on the face
and asked him to get out.

I was terrified. I imagined Adam in his summer
jacket standing in the center of Warsaw and
freezing. I knew there was no chance to go to
bring him to our home, for at that time there
were no taxis and suburban buses didn't go. At
home, every driver had already drunk a glass of
alcohol, so nobody could go to the center. I
asked him, what I could do to help. He said,
that he would like to come back home. And
suddenly it occurred to me. Still, he had keys
to my flat. I told him, that after all he might go
back home. He thanked me and the next day
he welcomed me with a platter of fried
dumplings, which his mother had given him
when he was leaving their flat. She had at
least as much decency.

Since that moment we had lived together. We
spent New Year's Eve '97/98 in Mykonos. Also
then, I got to know closer Anvero, who had
serious problems with his parents, as well. It
came to the situation that I was taking care of
that teenager for quite a long time. I was
negotiating with his parents and at the same
time forcing him to continue studies at a
photography technical school. At some point,
he started to call me his father. There were
quite many of similar kids in my life. Later,
most of them disappointed me terribly.

„Give me your face, your soul and your heart... In return, you'll get the kick."

In 1998 I was working for the cultural and
social magazine "Puls Stolicy". I was writing
overages of interesting events related to
Warsaw, but I also wrote general social texts.

One day, we received information from the Polish Press Agency that the first in Poland reunion of homosexual persons was going to be held under the Zygmunt's Column. Around ten persons were to come there, who were to hide their faces behind a sheet of paper with their jobs written there. In this way, the organizers wanted to prove, that gays and lesbians were present in our society and they had worked in various jobs. The managing editor of the department assigned a press photographer to me and ordered me to go there and make coverage.

So, we went there.

At the entrance to the Castle Square, under the Zygmunt's Column, we saw a big crowd of journalists. Though, it was still about half an hour before the beginning of the happening, the reporters' company turned up. When we came nearer, we saw that there were two boys nervously looking around standing on the steps of the monument. "Where are those ten courageous homosexuals?" I thought to myself.

Time was passing implacably, the reporters started to become impatient and I noticed that the boys were more and more nervous. Finally, I came up to them asked them, when they were going to start. "In a moment," the older one answered. "And where is the rest?" "Probably, there will be no one else." I wondered for a while and I came to a conclusion that two masked boys would look idiotic in the photos. I shared my doubts with the organizers. They shrugged their shoulders and said that they could do nothing about it. People were afraid that someone might recognize them even behind the mask.

"Damn it!" I thought.

I was a gay, but outside my circle, nobody knew about that. Admittedly, I was the first at the college to discuss writing a paper for Bachelor's Degree about gay press, but that didn't mean that I was a homosexual. Nobody from the editorial office has ever asked me about my private life. And all of a sudden, I was to witness someone, who wanted to show that life in hiding wasn't so good. And I was to keep away and describe that. Could I afford doing that? Maybe yes, but then, would I still be myself?

I don't know, what pushed me into that. Was it an impulse of the moment or maybe some inner need to stop living in a closet? I am not able to answer this question today. But at that moment I was determined. I gave my jacket to my surprised press photographer and I went up to the boys. "Give me sunglasses, a cap and a scarf. I started to write quickly in a sheet of paper: "I'm a reporter."

There weren't enough space on the paper to write. That's why in all those pictures you could see me signed "I'm a report." Cameras started to snap, video cameras were set in motion. I saw consternation in the faces of my colleagues by a trade. Here, one of them decided to break taboo. He wanted to show that there were homosexuals among them. After having read an appeal, we came apart. One of the journalists from Życie Warszawy came up to me and congratulated me on courage. I didn't know then, what I had really done. Together with the reporter, we came back to the editorial office, where I wrote coverage, which was to never be published.

The next day, I found an issue of the Gazeta Wyborcza on my desk. In the first page of the capital supplement there was a picture of me. A few minutes later, the editor-in-chief asked me to come to his office and informed me that I couldn't work for him any longer that I overstepped the mark.

In that way, I became out of work. For the next few days, I was getting calls from friends, who were asking me if it was really me in that picture, and they congratulated me and kept their fingers crossed for me. I believed that I would find a job in another editorial office. The time proved how wrong I had been.

Till the end of 1998 I lived in hope, that soon a stir would be over and I would catch hold in a publishing house. Though, every editorial office I applied for rejected me under flimsy pretext. Only in Gazeta Wyborcza, the person who interviewed me had enough courage to tell me the whole truth. Nobody wanted to hire an openly gay person. The things in theatre were similar.

After the event I stopped to get offers of figuration in the Powszechny theatre. I remember the conversation I had with the administrative manager very well. He told me that he couldn't hire an openly gay person. "For God's sake," I said. "*But half of your actors are gays.*" "*Yes, but they don't admit that on TV.*" In this way, my adventure with professional theatre came to an end. Also, I left Parabuch in the atmosphere of conflict. We weren't able to understand each other, as we used to do before. Something was missing, something came to a finish.

Though, I didn't care about it too much, for at my home, there was still the Public Youth Academy's office, so my more or less regular income made it possible to make a living.

A few days before the next Christmas, a discussion about preparation for the feast appeared on IRC. Also then, one of our friends from Bielsko Biała started to complain about his company, which sent him to Warsaw on the Christmas Vigil to see to something and he wouldn't be able to come back to his family town on time. I suggested that he might spend that time at my home instead of a hotel. He and the rest liked the idea. We decided to extend the concept and invite everybody who didn't quite have any idea where to go and what to do on that day.

It so happened, that we had supper at my mum's earlier than usual, cause both grandmas had to be transported back home. So, I was to be at home at 21 already. We decided to invite the solitary people at 21:30.

On that day at 14:00 somebody knocked on my door. I opened and saw a huge Christmas tree, behind which Szomiz was hidden. Szomiz was that friend from Bielsko Biała. After I came back from the family supper, we were waiting for the rest of the guests. To our surprise, more than 10 people arrived. Even those, who normally used to spend that evening with their families, after an official part of the Vigil, slipped away out to join us. Everyone had brought something to eat. Some of the dishes were quite weird as for a traditional Christmas Vigil, like for example French fish soup or salads with frutti di mare. Also, there was enough alcohol. Accounts from that event were fervently commented on IRC and we decided to repeat the whole thing the next year. In this way, a tradition of Christmas Vigil's supper for solitary gays and lesbians was born. Anyway, I've been cultivating it to this day.

We were spending the New Years Eve traditionally on a tour of the clubs. At that time, the owners of the clubs hadn't been concerned only about a quick profit, yet. So, you could make a tour of all the popular gay clubs in the capital for relatively not much money. The Mykonos, which was still gaining popularity, had a great problem with receiving all the people who wanted to enter, so still before midnight, we moved to the Paradise, where we were celebrating till morning. We reached home in an enlarged team, as usual. I disposed additional beds. We felt like one great family. That state was to last for a few more years.

The following year brought many changes.
I decided to make a serious decision concerning the next step towards independence. I established a company. Terra Incognita was to work at publishing the "Leser" and to provide advertising service for the Public Youth Academy and for an arising training company owned by Jacek and Dorota. I entrusted Adam, who had some experience of working for an advertising agency. I looked ahead confidently and didn't realize that future was preparing a bitter surprise for me.

At first, the "Leser" collapsed. The college, which was publishing its own magazine "Twarze", was no longer interested in supporting a black and white student bulletin printed in offset. Also, "Leser" didn't attract any advertisers, so after having published a few issues, I resigned from that activity. We focused on the advertising part. Our first serious order was publishing a training brochure for the Public Youth Academy. We prepared it at home working on two computers and racing against time. The result was not quite ravishing, but we were happy anyway. After that order, my mum arranged for us a regular order from the "Pracownia TROP", the Jakubowkis' company. We were to buy advertising space in the Gazeta Wyborcza for them. It ensured quite a regular income for us. I entrusted book-keeping service to my father's partner, Magda. At the same time, I trusted Adam boundlessly and I gave him total accesses to the company bank account. As time has proved, I was to pay a steep price for the two decisions.

But before it came to that, we gave a shelter to Anvero, who still couldn't come to terms with his parents. Inwardly, I counted that with time he would start working with us. At first, he seamed to be very willing to do that. When Adam succeeded in starting cooperation with a company I.N.N.A. from Poznań, we were in seventh heaven. The company was providing a producer of condoms with an advertising service. The producer wanted to carry out in Poland an advertising campaign directed to the gay society. In those times, that was equal to a revolution. The negotiations were advanced and Adam was visiting Poznań often to discuss the details. At one moment, a message came, that I should appear there in person to settle various questions of the contract. We made an appointment. Unluckily, one day before, the first in Warsaw reunion of the #gaypl was to be held. I agreed with Anvero, who was to go to

Poznań with me, that we would go to the party and in the morning we would take the first train to Poznań and go. Because it was a carnival, we were to put on funny costumes. So, we decked ourselves out as we could. I remember that one of worth mentioning elements of our disguise were tons of brocade and silver paint that we put on our faces and hair.

We came back from the party very late at night and not quite in a state suitable for going away. Of course, when going to sleep we didn't worry about careful cleaning off the make-up. In the morning, when I was trying to wake up Anvero, a wild row started. My "son" wasn't going to go away with me not for love or money. We were screaming at one another louder and louder, until we stood in front of each other yelling like crazy. When we both took a break to catch a breath, we noticed a cloud of brocade falling down on the floor around us. "*Oh, yeah,*" Anvero observed resigned. "*Like fucking fairies.*" We looked at each other and both burst out laughing. I went to Poznań alone.

In the meantime, someone appeared in my life. Of course, we met thanks to the Internet. Michał was from Wrocław and he was a high priest of the Order of Brothers and Sisters Politheists, the first in Poland religious association, which granted marriage to homosexual couples. It was thanks to him, that my interest in parapsychology entered the higher dimension. And at the same time, the faith principles professed by their church were soaked through ecumenism so much, that I had no problem with finding myself there. I had never joined that church, but, I was their supporter until the year 2000.

Not only similar attitudes towards faith united me and Michał. There was something more. We had made quite a successful couple for 6 months. He was accepted by my friends and many times he was coming to me from Wrocław with bags filled with food. He maintained that meat from his parts tasted completely different. He was an educated cook and a waiter. And I must admit he cooked superbly. I learned many great dishes from him. Anvero, who was his namesake, called him Teddy Bear or mum. He preferred to call himself Black Widow. Our relationship broke up mainly because of the distance and conflict of characters, though I recall him with a big sentiment.

In the second half of the year Adam moved to his new partner living near Warsaw. The situation between us wasn't very good. My accounts started not to square. At the same time, Adam started to become more and more nervous. At first, I and Ula were worried about his health, but subsequent medical tests showed that he was all right. But something was brewing. When he finally completely moved from my flat, many overdue invoices started to flood in to the office. Toward the end of the year, to my horror I understood that I stood on the brink of bankruptcy. Arrears together with percentage reached a dizzy sum of twenty eight thousand zlotys. I didn't have any other way out and I had to ask mum for help. We took my accounting from my father's partner and not before then a real tragedy began.

As if the overdue invoices and growing debt weren't enough, my father's partner was keeping the accounts in a completely careless way. If not my mum's help, I would have never managed to make everything clear. At the beginning of the year 2000, Terra Incognita suspended activity to come back again after a dozen or so months as a company organizing shows.

Though, before I got involved in the world of theatre and the stage again, I took up various jobs. I was a bartender and even a stripper.
I started dancing on the go-go stage by complete accident.

Are you not happy that we don't have abortion problem?

Szymon Niemiec naked? That's something new...

In the Mykonos club another reunion of the #gaypl was to be held. It was to be a first rate party. When I entered the club, it was difficult to find enough room to stand there. Everyone had a label with nicks from the channel. The atmosphere was even hotter, for at midnight there was to be a dance show performed by a hired stripper. Half an hour before the performance, I spotted Mormi, the main organizer of the reunion, who was crowding through in my direction with terror in his eyes. When he got to me, he told me in a stage whisper, that the stripper hadn't arrived. He asked me, what he should do. Everybody knew me as a person, who was familiar with the stage. I suggested that he should organize a quick competition for an amateur striptease. Something like, the one who would do that better, will get a reward. Our conversation was heard by one of the editors from the "Gejzer" magazine published by PinkPress, who was present at the reunion. He came up to us and offered that one of the rewards may be a yearly subscription of the "Gejzer" magazine. Another reward, a bottle of vodka, was offered by the owners of the club.

Midnight struck and the company gathered in a hall downstairs where in the middle of the tiled floor was a dancing pipe. We were thronging under the walls and waiting for the competition to begin. A girl, one of the administrators of the channel entered the improvised stage and announced the competition. She invited volunteers. I was standing in the first line and I was trying hard not to look into the eyes of the main organizer, who was standing just in front of me. But it didn't help. There were no volunteers. Five minutes passed and I glanced at Mormi. That was a mistake. His eyes were begging me: "Teeechniii... pleeeese... heeeelp."

I had only one beer, so I was thinking still soberly. In my head one thought arose. What is there to loose? Basically nothing.

I took a deep breath and entered the middle of the stage. People applauded me and after a while another competitor volunteered. We chose the music and began the show. Though, before we started dancing, the witch, who was running the show, whispered into our ears: "*But, gentlemen, not to the end.*"

We were dancing to the rhythm of a sharp music and we were freeing ourselves from successive parts of clothing at the same time watching the audience and observing each other. I had a bigger stage experience, so, as opposed to my opponent, I didn't focus on two or three people from the audience, but I was trying to dance around the whole circle. One moment, we remained only in underwear. And again, by accident, I had the advantage over my competitor. He was wearing normal briefs, and I had tight boxers. Thanks to that, at the moment when he started to hesitate what to do, I could still dance while rolling the boxers up on my body. Suddenly, I noticed that the other dancing guy in desperation started to strip off his underwear. I thought to myself, if he could, why couldn't I? And I slid the boxers down onto the floor. The audience started to uproar and cheer and we, escorted by the Witch, vanished in a provisional dressing-room arranged in a darkroom.

After we got dressed and went out, it appeared that I won. That was beginning of my acquaintance with Krzysiek Garwałtowski from PinkPress and my later cooperation with that publishing house.

In those days, I was still very young, I had a shapely body and short hair, which I bleached radically white. In ultraviolet light it looked amazing.

Some time later Mykonos was moved to the other end of Warsaw. I was lucky, for the new club was located a few bus stops from me. I started to be there frequently. Though, the change of localization and closing the club at Koźla Street, made the clubbing rhythm of the gay capital city totally broke. The people divided into admirers of the new Mykonos, lovers of the Paradise and frequent visitors of the Fantom, which was the oldest sex club with sauna in Poland.

At the same time, I landed in a hospital for the first time. Stress, unhealthy diet, and cigarettes caused in me an ulcerous illness. One evening, after quite a stormy parting with one of my partners, I started to feel a sudden pain below my ribcage. Hour after hour I was feeling worse and worse. Finally, I called for an ambulance. I was admitted to the hospital ward at Stępińska Street with a diagnosis of an ulcerous illness of duodenum. I spent there two weeks and observed the hospital life. The ward, I was staying, was called a dying house by my co-patients. It wasn't unfounded, for every night in front of our eyes the hospital attendants were carrying away at least one deceased. Luckily, my disease wasn't very serious and after 14 days I was discharged and could go back home. Since then, my duodenum reminds me about itself twice a year.

Behind the rainbow bar...

As a bartender I used to work in two places. The first was the Amigo, an infamous club near the Plac Trzech Krzyży, where I had worked for two months making the Internet site for the club's owners and working behind the bar. Though, when the owners, incited by one of the bartenders, wanted to deceive me on the payday, a big row started. I got a few blows from mafia people, called by them. From my working there I remember only two nice happenings. I met there two people. One of them was the oldest DJ I knew, who played the music at the requests of patrons, so everyone who came to the Amigo could hear exactly what he desired. He got sacked from the club a few days before me. The other one was a boy working as a prostitute. He came for a coffee one day just after we opened. We started to talk, for there were not many clients that day and he stayed there till we closed. I heard many interesting things about male prostitutes in Poland. He was telling me about their clients, about mafia collecting tributes, and about prison. He was a talker and his well built body was spoilt only with prison tattoos on his hands. That night I learned that a man selling his body for money was still a human being.

That was a very important experience for me.

After that infamous adventure with the Amigo, which was shut down soon after I left, I started to work as a bartender in the new Mykonos. Unfortunately, I was privileged to work there only for a month. I came there at the moment, when a cloud was on the horizon for the owners of the club. The protests of the residents, groups of drunken blockers gathering near the club and other problems influenced the owners to close the Mykonos down. We all felt sorry about that. For those looking for fun, there was only the Paradise club remaining.

Soon, the year two thousand was to be another turning point in life of the homosexual milieu in Poland.

Ambassador without underwear...

The biggest pornographic publishing house, which published "Nowy Men" and "Gejzer," decided to organize a great event, thanks to which gays would have a chance for outing. They had contacts with the International Lesbian & Gay Culture Network. This was a unique chance to invite to Poland the organizers of the III World Culture Conference of Gays and Lesbians. Even a sponsor occurred in the form of Lufthansa, which promised to offer free flights to the guests from abroad. The organizers announced in mainstream press and in the gay websites, that they were looking for volunteers to attend the events and the foreign guests. Straight away, I volunteered to Marek Tamborski, who was responsible for the organization of the event. And I became a volunteer.

At our first meeting it appeared, that apart from me, there were only my acquaintances. Thus, Marek charged me with coordination of the volunteers. We took attendance to the foreign guests, and service at the events upon ourselves.

The program was filled up with meetings, concerts and conferences. In total, there were over 200 guests from 20 countries. One of the most moving moments was the meetings in the former extermination camp Oświęcim, where the delegation from Sweden presented the management of the museum with the Orfeo Iris Award, commemorating places of extermination of homosexuals. The other moving moment was a concert of women violinists from Finland, who under the extermination wall made a catching appeal for peace.

The last two days of the conference were to be devoted mainly to fun. On the last day before the end, the Poland Championship of Amateur Strippers was planned. On the day of the competition, it appeared that nobody had applied. Of course, the organizers could hire boys from an agency, but they didn't want them to look too professional. Marek Tamborski came to me and asked if I was going to agree to make a show. I was quite shocked for I had done that only once in my life, at that reunion, where the audience wasn't so big. And there, it was to be a show in front of a big international audience. I agreed under one condition that he would find at least one more person for the competition.

Eventually, one more participant applied for the competition, apart from me. The two remaining were hired by the PinkPress from an agency. After I had seen them at a rehearsal, I knew that I didn't have a slightest chance to win. Then I thought, that if I couldn't be the best, let me at least catch the audience's eye with originality. I knew that the boys from the agency weren't going to show anything new, except a standard dance without clothes. I came back home to change and in my wardrobe I found my leather trousers, military boots, some leather accessories and an old habit. I also took with me my then favorite E Nomine's record. During the next few hours, I worked out a number very controversial in its content. I decided to enter the stage dressed in a habit, under which I was wearing a uniformed as for sadomasochistic practices. I had some of those toys at home, for I had used them before for the cabaret shows.

My opponent, who applied for the competition himself, also bet on originality and he performed a strip-tease dressed as a women.

I remember an ovation made by the audience, when I entered the stage. People were reacting very spontaneously and though I was trying not to show everything, I met with hot applause.

During the break between the end of the show and the announcement of the results, Bill Schiller, a coordinator of culture ambassadors of the ILGCN, run up to me and started to congratulate me rapidly. Then, he asked me, if I wouldn't like to become an Ambassador of the Polish Culture attached to the ILGCN. I was completely shocked. At that moment, I didn't understand why my show arose such ravishment in the western guests. Marek Tamborski uncovered that secret to me.

It occurred, that a few days before, already during our conference, the pope John Paul II delivered a very critical speech on homosexuality. Our western guests understood my performance as a symbol of homosexuality freeing itself from the bonds of Catholicism.

When Bill Schiller got to know, that I was a theatrical instructor, and one of the first persons in Poland, who publicly admitted their sexual orientation, he started to persuade me to accept the title even more fervently. I had never been active in any gay organization and I didn't know, what followed from that title. I was afraid to accept it, but finally, I came to a conclusion, that it couldn't do any harm to me, anyway.

The next day, during a formal meeting finishing the conference, Bill read off a ILGCN's resolution about appointment of new ambassadors. In that way, I became the Ambassador of the Polish Culture attached to the ILGCN. Photographs from that event were published later in the Gejzer magazine and that is the only trace that had been left after the last strip-tease in my career.

At the conference, I also met the Reverend Ernest Ivanovs, a pastor of the Free Reformed Church in Latwia. Ernest came to Poland with his partner, but already at the conference you could see that the relation between them was tense. They split just before their leaving for Ryga.

Most of the foreign guests were staying the night at our homes and I had a privilege to take care of Ernest and his partner. Apart from them, two women from Latvia stayed in my flat. Some of the guests had to sleep on the mattresses on the floor, but nobody cared. We were joined by a common initiative of the conference and with an international kind of solidarity. We were spending our free time on long talks and discussions. Ernest was a great conversationalist. An open, honest and very warm way he spoke.

At some moment, when talking about the God, depicted both by a Christian and metaphysical grasp, we came to a conclusion, that really we were tasking about the same God calling Him with different names. That conclusion took root of a strong conviction about a need for ecumenism. The most important thing in that experience was the fact that Ernest didn't try to persuade me to come back to Christianity in either way. He didn't try to force anything. He respected my opinion and attitude toward life. I was really captivated by that.

Thanks to meeting Ernest, I started to think about my faith. I knew that coming back to the bosom of the Catholic Church wasn't an option for me. I just wouldn't be able to be a member of an organization, which openly discriminated against people of my orientation. I was working the problem through for another year.

In 2000 on the political scene, Robert Biedroń appeared. To be honest, he rather not appeared, but was shown. The Democratic Left Alliance (SLD) began to notice a presence of homosexual persons and needed a symbol, which would associate them with those circles. Prominent heterosexual politics didn't present a sufficiently attractive breeding-ground for media, so the party invented a new one. Robert emerged out of nowhere. Before that, nobody knew him in the society, and suddenly he appeared as the first openly member of the party. For that he got then an award of a Rainbow Laurels. It's worth mentioning at that point, that that was a precedent in the history of the award. The main assumption was to award the Rainbow Laurel exclusively to the heterosexual persons for their contribution to the fight for minority rights. But because already then the awarding chapter was strongly related to the left wing, they candidacy of Robert was forced through and he got his statuette during an honorable gala at the Rampa theatre.

Meanwhile, holidays had passed. I portioned my time between home and the Paradise. At that time, we had a group of friends there, and we met practically every day. At some point, the Paradise had even organized breakfasts in the form of a buffet for their guests. For me that was the time of meeting new people. Some of them were to become my close friends. With some of them, a joined struggle for equal rights for everyone had joined me.

My emotional life was lying fallow. To tell you the truth, I was dating some men from time to time, but usually the matters didn't go beyond the question of bed.

Enter Mother Theresa for the Fags...

I've been always treated by my peers as if I was older. For some of them I was a kind of an oracle and they turned to me with every problem. At some point, even an epithet arose, which I started to use to call myself Mother Theresa for the Fags. It's not important, who first used that name to describe me. The fact was that when a young gay ran away from home, the police called me asking if I didn't see him by chance or if I didn't know if he was seen in the clubs. A few times the police together with parents took away such a culprit from my flat. Though, I've never had any problems caused by that fact. The officers were grateful to me for making their job easier. Also, the parents didn't quite have any reason to complain, for I had always imposed a condition to all the runaways that they could stay at my home for the price of informing their parents. Usually, I also took up negotiations between the family and the gay, who either revealed himself or were forced to reveal. I had experience from my own home. Besides, there was always a kind of a peace in me, thanks to which I was able to overcome sometimes extreme emotions. At times, I felt proud, that forty year olds were listening to a boy many years younger than them, who explained to them that their child didn't suddenly become bad, only for the reason that he told them the truth. Some of those parents became open to that extend that they started to visit the clubs with us.

Meanwhile, during our meetings in the Paradise, a group of close friends crystallized. At some point that group started to issue a black and white monthly newsletter "Outsider," later given away for free in the Paradise. The "Outsider" was copied on a Xerox machine at work by Robert Ciepiela, known to all of us as Lady Vicky. Since, I moved in the circles of artists-mimics. Thus, in our group were Lady Vicky and Lady Desdemona. The Paradise became a place of our meetings also because it was the first club in Warsaw offering an open, big stage with lighting and sound system necessary for the drag queens' shows. Among us there were also women, among others, a wonderful artist-photographer Agata Gorządek. With time, our group was growing bigger, there were new people coming, which whom we were working, making friends and having fun. New relationships, couples and loves were born. Though, I was still alone.

Behind me, I had many sexual affairs, recollections of which are disgusting to me today. I must admit, that at a certain point, I repent, I used to believe in a stereotype of a gay having a different partner every day. I even tried to live that way, but soon I understood that that kind of life doesn't suit me. It was boring and didn't give me any satisfaction.

One of such affairs was to influence my life for years.

Vacation 2000 was drawing to an end. Fall was at hand. One day, I was spending my time in one of the newly created gay chats and I got a private message from someone, who was looking for someone for having sex. I had hesitated for a while, but then I decided, that basically, I had nothing to loose. We exchanged out photographs and we started to make a factual appointment. Then, he wrote, that his friend felt like doing that in a triangle. I didn't see the photo of that other boy, but I said yes and invited them to my place. After more or less an hour, they arrived.

When I opened the door, I saw the man I made an appointment with going first and Krzysiek, who was following him. Having seen him, I already knew, I wouldn't regret my decision about our meeting. Though, because we agreed to make sex in triangle, after a short conversation while drinking tea, we moved to the bedroom. While I don't remember the body of the man accompanying us, I still treasure in my memory the picture of naked Krzysiek. Especially, a vision of a tattoo in his groin sank in my memory. That small rainbow hued flag was his distinctive feature as he admitted many weeks later.

You couldn't say the sex that night was successful. After several minutes of intensive petting, Krzysiek excused us and left us and vanished in the other room. We wouldn't care too much, if we didn't hear him weeping from behind the wall. After a moment we were by his side.

When I think about that now, I must admit, it must have been quite a comical sight. The two naked men sitting on the sofa and trying to comfort the third one weeping, already half dressed. I have to admit, that Krzysiek always knew, how to attract everybody's attention.

We already knew that sex that night would come to nothing. So we drunk another tea, exchanged our phone numbers and said good-bye. A few days later, I contacted Krzysiek proposing a meeting. That was an innocent coffee, which we repeated a few days later developing that with a supper with breakfast. When Krzysiek was telling me about himself, he unfolded a vision of a responsible, and successful and experienced man. We were slowly discovering our common features. We both liked to cook. We were thinking about stabilization.

Gradually, nights started to prolong to a few days meetings. Finally, October 2000 came. Because already then, I had quite a big circle of friends, I was planning to organize my birthday party in a club. That was more convenient than inviting everybody to home, cost less and was easier to herd. That's why, on the fifth of October 2000, together with Krzysiek, we appeared in Paradise, and where tables laid with bottles of champagne awaited us.

Many of my friends turned up and the party began.

I appeared with Krzysiek at my clubs. Of course, everybody wanted to know, if we were a couple. That night we thought that over and decided there was no sense in deceiving each other any longer. We were in a relationship. We acknowledged that officially at that party.

At that time I was working as an archivist in an erotic publishing house PinkPress. That was the only job in a way related in my profession that I could get. As an openly gay person, who from time to time appeared in various TV programs and in press, I didn't have a chance to find a job as a journalist. Even the most controversial papers weren't interested in hiring an individual, who in the public awareness was perceived as an openly gay person. Those first years barred from professional journalism were especially painful to me. I learned then to repeat to myself, that there will come a time for everything.

My work for the PinkPress consisted mainly in cataloguing and describing photos from the electronic archives, but because of a constant rotation of the staff, I was frequently asked for help in writing texts, short stories and answers for the letters form readers in the Agony Column.

With time, I started to take part in the production of the photo sessions as a stylist and the photograph's assistant. Thanks to working with Adam Miłosz, I've learned many tricks when making photos of a naked body, which appeared to be useful later, at my work for the models' agency and working as a independent photographer.

With time, the editors started to order me to write reports from various events. I was attending some of them together with Krzysiek. In that way, one day we landed at an International Fair of Tattoo, in which also our female models took part. A thought about making a tattoo absorbed my thoughts before, but I never found either time or enough motivation. I always wanted to have a tattoo that would be different from all the other ones that I had seen on the other people's bodies before. I didn't want anything ordinary or traditional. Having read many elaborations concerning tattoo, I noticed that many masters of that art stressed, that the tattoo should express its owner. It should emphasize and describe that person. It should become its part, because as you know, it is for the rest of your life. At the fair we were talking to many people and by accident we got to a stand of a tattoo salon from Gdańsk. That was the only stand, at which two young boys got interested in my idea and decided to realize it. We agreed that we would come back a few hours later to see a ready design. I approved the picture prepared by the boys and let them start working. More or less two hours later, a seven-colored picture of a bird bleeding a little appeared on my left buttock. Krzysiek liked the tattoo so much, that he immediately ordered its copy on his arm. The gentlemen fulfilled his request and I didn't expect then, that in a way I got connected with that man for ever. From that time, a few years passed and some colors of my decoration vanished, like Krzysiek from my life.

And more and more often I think about transforming that rainbow bird on my butt into something that would adjust to my personality again. What would that be this time? The time will show. Anyway, that rainbow little bird became my specific determinant. It's as if a tribal token, which connected me to the world of ideas, dreams and homosexuality, of course.

Some time later, I almost made the first porno film in my life. I wrote a screenplay, and the editorial staff got interested in it. I even managed to find the actors. Though, the whole thing appeared to be a great failure. Today I think that for me it was lucky stroke of fate. Though, making that porn produced an additional effect, which occurred a bit later. One of the actors who was to perform in the film was a boy from a little place near Wrocław. A few weeks after his visit in our studio, he called me and said that he was then in Warsaw and he would like to meet me.

I invited him home. He was a tall and very handsome dark-haired boy. Already standing in my doorway, he informed me that his father expelled him from home. I suggested that he should sit down. He refused. He was leaning his buttocks against the table and standing all the time, he told me his story, about how his father learned, that his son was gay. As a believing and practicing Catholic, what's more, working as a parish organist, he went to his parson for advice. That man ordered him to knock that foolery out of the son's head. The loyal parishioner listened to his shepherd and after coming home, he gave the son hell with help of a piano string. I didn't want to believe in that version of events, but the boy showed me his back. I understood why he didn't want to sit down. The skin on his back was literally cut into pieces. Only thanks to a doctor's intervention, and powerful painkillers, that poor boy was able to collect his emotions and run away from his place to the capital. That was one of the most difficult and painful cases of homophobia, that I dealt with. I tell that story always, when someone tries to make me believe, that homosexuals have an excellent life in our country. At that point I must stress, that it wasn't the only example of an attempt of "a forced healing," that I came across in my life.

And again in the light of the limelight...

After a few months of my work, the company decided to organize a Polish erotic fair. I was to take part in the event as one of many workers. During the fair I was backstage helping the actors and models performing, I was looking after the back where the artist could have a rest. The culminating point of the last day of the fair was to be an attempt of breaking a Sexual Record of Poland. The day before, a selection match for the contestants was held and I conducted that. It consisted mainly in checking if the men applying for the breaking of the record would be able to achieve and maintain erections. Two girls, who performed in the PinkPress productions, were helping them.

The breaking of the record itself was to be run by a popular new journalist. Someone mentioned Maciej Orłoś. Though, two hours before the beginning, Krzysiek Garwatowki came to me. He sat heavily in the backstage and said that we had a problem, because there was no master of ceremonies. He asked me, if I would agree to run the event. I asked what the payment was. He answered with a question, how much I would like to get. I suggested a large price hoping that he would give up. But he agreed to my conditions and ordered me to prepare myself. What else could I do? I went to the back to settle the details with the stage service, the main actress, women fluffers and the doctor, who was to watch over the course of the event. Later, it began.

For the first one hundred goes, I was still excited about what was happening on the stage. I was exclaiming subsequent tens with enthusiasm. Later, I felt only a growing disgust. When after a few days, I saw a material recorded at that event, and I kept in mind from it only my hoarse, dispassionate voice – NEXT, PLEASE. And from the whole happening, I also remember, that just after the breaking of a record had finished, I ran to the backstage like a shot to have a drink of vodka. Without that I wouldn't be able to retain my lunch in my stomach. For many days, I was haunted by the sight of that girl sitting in a gynecological chair receiving men one by one into her. When the next week my second name appeared in the Wprost weekly, that was a proverbial nail in my coffin. Under the pressure of mum am Krzysiek, I resigned from working for the PinkPress.

Though, before I finally sad goodbye to the publishing house, Sławek Starosta took me with his crew to Mińsk in Belarus. I went there as an Ambassador of the Polish Culture attached to the ILGCN. I didn't expect what I saw in that country. That was Poland from the times of Stalin.

Especially, two things are imprinted in my memory. The first one was the manner the authorities made short work of our festival of gay art. There were no bans or policing operation. Simply, at first the authorities cut off power in the district, in which the club we hired was located. And then, from day to day, they closed down the community center in which our conference was to be held. It was just an example of a law-abiding and unambiguous suppressing of the hostile propaganda. Finally, the lectures were held in a park. And the only reason, why the police didn't arrest us, was the fact that officially we gathered there to drink alcohol. Yes, in Belarus, drinking alcohol in public places is permitted.

The other fact, which I still remember from that trip, was the First Military Unit of Mińsk, the Belarusian gays called the Biggest Brothel of Europe. The name was not accidental, for I don't know any other European sexual agency hiring 2 000 of workers. How did that temple of delight function? In quite a simple way in fact. You just pulled up the main gate of the Unit, and left a note with an address and a description of your requirements at a gate-house. More or less after an hour, in your door a soldier reported, who stayed till dawn for the price of 20 dollars (an equivalent of their half a year's wages). You had to bring him back to the Unit before the morning assembly. Sławek had tested that system, and it fell to my lot to see the young soldier to the Unit. On our way back I bought him a plastic gilded watch at a market place. The boy was so happy, that he was ready to make sex with me in the street. Luckily, I managed to convince him, that such a token of was absolutely not necessary.

Belarus is also famous for cheap alcohol. That is typical for totalitarian countries, in which the authorities are perfectly aware, that the shops may be short of everything except vodka. Belarusian people don't buy drinks or glasses of vodka. A basic unit of alcohol is a bottle. Anyway, it wasn't worth buying a glass, for one glass of Absolute or Polish Sobieski cost the same as a bottle of a local alcohol. We came back from Belarus after a few days, on our way back having gone through an unpleasant adventure at the border. A customs official didn't want to let me leave the country. He claimed that I had a forged passport. Finally, I showed him my Identification Card and that convinced him, that I was I. When I think about that now, I come to a conclusion that he just counted on a bribe, which in that reality was as natural as bread and vodka.

After I returned again, I plunged in the world of the Polish little hell.

In December 2000 for the first time me and Krzysiek appeared in a Polish public TV. That was a live program, aired at 22:30 on the night before the Polish presidential election. The topic of the discussion was a question if homosexual persons should have right to adopt children. Also then I met Jurek Nasierowski, one of the most colorful figures of the gay society of the previous system. Gays didn't exist in the comprehension of media. We were a sensation, invited to the television to fulfill in the mandatory 24 hours pre-election news coverage silence.

I remember, that after the recording, a young boy dressed in black with a big silver cross in his chest came up to us, when we were standing in the corridor. In a lapel of his black suit he had stack a sign of Conservative-Liberal Association "KoLiber". He asked me if he could talk to me for a while. When I agreed, he whispered very excited: *"You know, I'm a homosexual, as well. But I'm getting treatment. A priest helped me and now I'm aspiring to priesthood."* I was speechless. He looked 18 or 19 years old. I looked deep into his eyes and I saw a fearful sadness in them. That kid was so terribly lonely and frightened, that he decided to harm himself only in order to be accepted. I've often wondered how many of such boys got to the "KoLiber" or to the All-Polish Youth (MW), when looking for acceptation through denying themselves.

That late night program on the first public television channel was a specific turning point in the life of me and Krzysiek. Though it didn't have a big viewership, it provoked a considerable interest in our relationship by others. With time, invitations for TV programs and interviews in press started to arrive to us.

In 2000 I didn't work for any theatre and my stage life was surviving a kind of stagnation. From time to time, me and Krzysiek took liberty of tomfoolery in clubs on the occasion of Halloween or some costume parties, but those were not either official or professional shows. That situation was to change in December, when in the Paradise the first charity concert for children with HIV/AIDS was held. Already in November, when the first preparations began, the main organizer, Robert Łukasik, asked me if I would like to make a show on the stage. It turned out, that there were not enough Drag Queen artists, who'd wanted to perform for free. After a moment of hesitation, I agreed and together with a few other artists I started to prepare a show.

Contrary to popular opinion, a drag queen doesn't consist just in dressing yourself as a woman and entering the stage. A man, who is taking up that job, has to be not only a master of actor's technique, but also a great sense of style and humor. Of course, there are many drag queens, who think differently. Many gays think that it's enough to put on a dress and a bra stuffed with socks, a wig and stilettos to become a drag queen. We see them on various stages in clubs, where they make an effort to make the audience laugh. Some of them are even successful at that. Though, true artists may be easily recognized. Their dresses are elaborated, their make-up is made with professional stage cosmetics, and you won't have any doubts that he devoted many hours to choreography. The similar thing is with selection of their repertoire. Working as an artist-parodist is a hard work only the best ones stay on the stage for longer. Those, who treat that only as an entertainment leave the stage soon and never, come back.

During my first performance the biggest problem posed the choice of repertoire. Together with the rest of the artists we prepared a common final number from the repertoire of Madonna and we began holding rehearsals. The concert was divided into two parts. The first one, a gala concert, was held on Thursday, 30th of November. A great surprise for us was a presence of the Polish Republic's President's wife, Mrs. Jolanta

Kwasniewski. She made an extremely positive impression on us. And though she didn't stay long at the club, she managed to prove, that she felt free and unconstrained by the fact that she was in a gay club. To tell you the truth, the press writing a short report from the event, didn't say a word about the fact, that the Paradise was a club for homosexual persons. Simply, there was no such a topic. Mrs. Jolanta Kwaśniewska made a positive impression also because of the way she was dressed, which was perfectly matching the club atmosphere. The leather jacket and chic trousers showed the leeway and elegance of that best Polish First Lady.

Our show took place on Sunday, 3rd of December, was a genuine success. When I look at the pictures from that day, I'm not able to recognize myself. Indeed, the girls from a make-up studio did a good job. I landed at a casting of a photo model agency Studio Seklecki in Warsaw. After a shot interview with Iza, a co-owner of the agency, we agreed that we would start cooperation. I was to work there not only as a model, but also as an instructor.

For the next few years I was holding courses for male and female models and photo models. I dealt with a few hundred young people, who wanted to taste fame and the limelight. Though, very few of them managed to come to the top of the modeling business. In the agency I was treated with fear. Male and female models were afraid of me; I was a terribly demanding instructor. I knew that only the most persistent of them had any chance at castings. Everyone who had taken part in my workshop later had to take an examination in front of a video camera and an examination board. Though, the rest of the members of the board used to quite understand, everyone who stood face to face with me knew that they couldn't count on any concessions. I didn't spare one of the later finalists of the program IDOL, who only when appeared at our agency, at once he wanted to be a star. He was terribly disappointed, that his poor abilities didn't find any of my understanding. After his show in the Idol finale TV, I sent him an e-mail with compliments. He didn't answer, but that didn't surprise me. I'm sure that he doesn't have nice memories of me. Working for the agency used to take me most of the time, the rest of which I was trying to divide into social work and private life. I started to grow my hair, for Iza told me, that there was a demand for long haired models. I was selected for a photo session in the role of Jesus. It came quite easy to me, when you take into consideration, that my hair already reached shoulder length, and Iza with help of the make-up girls, was capable of conjuring wonders out of wax and paint. In the pictures, I looked like the Man of Nazareth. Before the session, we made a deal with Iza, that in exchange for posing, I would get money or equivalent on clothes from Arkadius. A few days after the session, I got a message, that the pictures wouldn't be used. I forgot about the whole thing until one day, when passing by Arkadius's boutique in the center of Warsaw, I saw myself looking at me from a poster. Not only were my pictures hanging in the boutique, each of them was also bearing a price tag. When I called the agency to learn what was going on, they informed me, that that was none of my business and since I didn't have any contract signed with them, I might vindicate my rights at the photographer's. While the photographer himself was very confused, for he knew, that the agency earned quite a lot of money thanks to those pictures. Everything ended with a solemn promise not to have anything to do with the Sekleckis.

I managed to learn very many tricks, which I could later use at the work of a photographer. Having tasted the role of an artist-parodist, I started to perform regularly. In the beginning I worked with a company of other drag queens and later alone. With time, Krzysiek joined me. At first, he performed as a man, but after a few months, from day to day; we exchanged our roles with each other. From that moment, I performed only as an announcer. We wanted to prove that a drag queen's show was not just only entering the stage in woman's clothes and feigning singing. We managed to create a real cabaret with texts, songs and complicated choreographic forms. Our greatest success was a program "Tych lat nie odda nikt" telling about the years of the past political system.

Another protest against our government Sir!

In October 2000 at the Paradise nightclub, as usual, a group of friends gathered to gossip about the things, that was who, to whom, for what and why. Time was passing away cheerfully, by beer and chips, when somebody observed that that was nice that I had a title of an ambassador, but either way, I could do nothing with that, for there was no ILGCN in Poland.

"Why not?" I asked. For the next 6 years I rebuked myself for not curbing my tongue at that moment. It began in an innocent way from an idea to create a Polish division of the ILGCN. Though, according to the registration regulations of those times, that wasn't possible. You had to register a Polish association. In addition, the National Court Register didn't exist yet, and the whole procedure was to be conducted in a normal district court. The first obstacle occurred to be the name of the association. The amiable women officials informed us, that the association had to be registered under a polish name, for the law didn't assume possibility of existence of Polish non-governmental organizations bearing foreign names. When correcting the charter in a slapdash way, we made a mistake when translating the International Lesbian & Gay Culture Network in Poland into the Międzynarodowe Stowarzyszenie Gejów i Lesbijek na Rzecz Kultury w Polsce . Nobody noticed that we replaced gays with lesbians until Agata Gorządek, one of the first women in the association, called our attention to that. Unfortunately, it was too late for a change. The founding committee consisted of 4 persons. Apart from them, 20 founding members signed the application form for founding. Most of them signed the motion only in order to allow the organization to be created. The future proved that that style of founding the non-governmental organization wasn't the most fortunate idea.

The year 2001, was another critical point for the homosexual circles in Poland. Towards the end of February I got an e-mail from the organizers of an annual feminist demonstration "Manifa," who wanted to ask, if the homosexual circles would like to present themselves at their demonstration. We thought that over together with Krzysiek and decided that we should be present there.

Then, it turned out, that in the entire country of Poland there wasn't a single rainbow hued flag, under which we could march. We started a feverish search. Around a week before the Manifa, we found ourselves in a shop with propaganda articles in Warsaw, where we got to know, that though they didn't have a rainbow hued flag on the stock, they could make it for our order. The sewing of the flag cost us 150 zloty. We covered the whole city in search for materials of the right colors. We were looking for them till the last moment, and we couldn't find orange. Finally, we were so desperate, that we decided to replace orange with gold. In this way, the first rainbow flag, which appeared in the streets of Warsaw had improper colors.

At the Manifa, every now and again, journalists were coming up to us. At first, we didn't understand, why they were asking us if the "Społem" Cooperative Society was supporting feminists. Not until a reporter from the Gazeta Wyborcza reminded us of the fact, that a rainbow hued flag was a symbol of that Polish company.

Though, with a difference, because their rainbow had seven colors, while ours had six. When we explained, who we were, everyone asked the same question: *"What do the gays had to do with women?"* That question was constantly asked at every feminist demonstration we took part in under our rainbow banner.

At that point, on the 8th of March 2001, none of us knew that there was another way for homosexual persons to spring up in the social space, which is the street. Our conviction was to change very soon.

A few weeks after the Manifa, we were sitting in the Paradise nightclub and watching a film, which one of the guests brought from Australia. That was a report from gay and lesbians parade in Sydney from the year 2000. We were watching those pictures spell-bound. There were thousands of colors, loud music and platforms with dancers, as from samba festival in Rio. Someone observed: *"What a pity, it's not possible at our country."* And then, I had to blurt out, as usual: *"Why not?"* I don't want to bore you with describing what was happening for the next few days. I only need to mention tons of documents, rules and regulations that we read together with Krzysiek looking for a possibility to let the gay and lesbians walk through the streets of Warsaw in the parade. There were a lot of "buts," but still more "against."

The name posed the basic problem. We didn't want to call our march a Parade of Gays and Lesbians, because we knew well, that the city wouldn't agree to allow for such a march. Besides, we didn't want our parade to gather solely homosexual persons, but everyone also, who met with injustice or social exclusion. Finally, one day, I woke up with the ready name. It was all about equality, right? So, why couldn't we call that the Equality Parade? Equality for everyone. In this way, the name was born. It's been used by media, politicians and also ordinary people to define marches of sexual minorities in Poland. It's not a Gay Pride, but Equality Parade.

By way of a debate, we came to a conclusion, that the only date, which guaranteed us approval of the march, was 1st of May. That was a traditional day of marches and the only day of the year, on which you didn't have to obtain any consents for occupation of one lane of the street. Thus, we submitted our parade at the town council. Since the ILGCN-Polska hadn't been registered officially, we had to submit the march as private persons. In that way, I became the first Manager of the Project Equality Parade. The documents landed at the offices and then it began.

On the Internet, there were three gay Portals at that time. There was an erotic gay.pl ran by PinkPress, the oldest gay site Inna Strona and a fresh information and dates Web portal Gejowo, which evolved form a private site. Gejowo became famous because of waging war with Inna Strona. Whatever IS did, it was immediately a subject of a critic on the Gejowo. So, you shouldn't be surprised, that when Inna Strona started to promote our parade, Gejowo pick IS to pieces. When Janusz Marchwiński, the editor-in-chief, wrote: *"Come to prove, that we exist!"* Rafał Nawrocki, the owner of Gejowo answered: *"It's not worth making a fool of yourself. Give it a miss."*

Of course, in the Warsaw circles, there were different opinions on the parade. Practically, nobody believed, that that might be a success. And because nobody believed in that, there was nobody, who would like to help. Finally, it turned out, that we were a group of 4 persons to organize a whole week event, which we eventually had to limit to a march. We wanted to print posters, but we had no money. We wanted a platform, but nobody wanted to help us.

Eventually, Agata Grządek made a project of leaflets, stickers for the public places and posters – black and white, to enable us to print them on Xerox machine. We were visiting the clubs with those posters begging the owners to let us hang them. Only few of them agreed. In the streets of the capital, maybe 300 posters appeared. And immediately they were removed by the city. One week before the parade we were desperate, for it seemed to us, that everything would collapse. And yet again, Inna Strona came to our invaluable help – it sent us two flags for free, and the owners of the Paradise club, who paid for a car with the sound system. In a warehouse "Adam," found a man who imported little rainbow flags from Germany and we purchased all the flags he had in stock. That meant all the 30 items. As if I had not enough nerves for me, a few days before the Parade, Michał Grochowiak turned to me. He wanted to make a documentary film about me as his work to get a pass and graduate the school. I agreed and they were following me for a few days with a cameraman and making a material about the way I lived. A film "Ambassador" was made of that. It is still available for viewing at some places.

The 1 May was inevitably approaching. The last day of April was cloudy and my heart was petrified, if the weather the next day would be nice. If it was raining, chances that anyone would come were equal to zero. Though, it appeared, that clearly someone up above must have liked us. 1st of May welcomed us with a hot weather and a beautiful sun of May.

The first step onto the rainbow...

Looking back, I can see myself standing alone in front of the St. Anne's Church at the Krakowskie Przedmieście Street. We oriented ourselves too late, that we wouldn't manage set off starting from the Zygmunt's Column, as we planned before. Simply, because a parking lot between the Castle Square and Krakowskie Przedmieście Street was tightly blocked up with cars and our machine with the sound system couldn't force our way through. So I sent Krzysiek under the Column to collect the people, who went there. And I stayed there standing alone under the rainbow flag under the church.

The first, who got any interest in me, were policemen, who after they made sure that I was an organizer of the march, quickly discussed with me the way of moving through the street. We were to set off at 14:00 sharp. We were on the spot at 13:00 and we were observing the people passing by. A question: "How many people will come?" was tormenting us. The closer 14:00 was, the more often the question was replaced by another question: "Will anyone come?" We didn't really like the idea to march as 4 persons following a car with a loud sound system.

A few minutes before 14:00, in front of our eyes a car appeared, from which 4 figures in disguise got out of the car. It turned out that our friends, who performed as drag queens, decided to support us. Thus, at the first Parade we were to have drag queens. When compared to the western parades, 4 artists was a very decent number, but anyway, that was something. Meanwhile, the people started to gather. From the direction of the Zygmunt's Column, Piotr Iknonowicz from the Polish Socialist Party came accompanied by Robert Biedroń. That last one probably didn't believe to the last moment, that we could succeed, because he was trying to keep aside. Besides, only at the moment, when we made a decision to start moving, it turned out that most of the participants were standing on the pavements waiting and observing, if anything was going to happen. When one of the most popular gay pop hits, that were "YMCA," came from the loudspeakers and reached the ear, people started to march behind us. With my trembling hands, I grasped a microphone connected by wire with a technician sitting inside the car. I welcomed everybody and invited them to a joined march. Finally, we set off.

For the first time we stopped opposite the Governor's Palace. I didn't have anything prepared. No speech, no slogans. Everything went spontaneously done. I managed to tack together a few sentences and we went on. I saw Robert Biedron's sour face, who was observing the journalists and cameras, which followed our every step. One moment, Sławek Starosta approached me and said: *"Can you see that? We managed to do that*!!!" Without stopping, we reached the Nicolaus Kopernik

Monument, where sour faces of the PPS members welcomed us. They were looking through the windows to see their chairman walking with homosexuals. At the sound of "Thank You For The Music" we dismissed the demonstration and came back home. But before that, I asked the police, how many of us were there. According to them, there were around 300 persons. How many of us were afraid to join the demonstration and was walking down the pavement? You can't tell. Though, all of us shared a feeling that we created the history. At home, I sat at the computer and checked my mail. Among many congratulation letters, the one from Krzysiek Garwatowski drew my attention. He informed me, that in the first gay parade in the world, which was held in New York, 150 persons took part. We felt drunk with joy.

On public TV not a word was said about us, and the next day some newspapers published short notices about our march. Whereas the gay Internet was in turmoil Inna Strona was writing about a great success, the Gejowo about a great failure. The Gay.pl maintained that they were a media patron and co-organizer of the success but this was not true. Bitter words poured in, but finally the issue was hushed up. At the same time, we got many warm letters form newly created lesbian and gay sites, which offered their help with organization of the next parade. We felt proud and able to face the whole world.

In June we got a paper from the court, which finally confirmed the registration of our association. From that moment, we could officially be present as the International Gay & Lesbian Culture Network in Poland. At the first general assembly of the association members, I was elected the president of the managing board and Krzysiek was elected the treasurer. Besides, Krzysiek was seeing to all the bureaucratic issues. He settled the VAT ID and REGON. Next, we opened a bank account and started to think about future operations.

The first logo of our association was created by Radek Oliwa from the IS. Anyway, from the very beginning, the Inna Strona was trying to help our associations as they could. Thanks to them, we received the space for or site on the server and e-mail boxes. At first, our site was very decent. But with time, we started cooperation with the founder of the first lesbian Web portal, Kara Auchemann. She decided to help us and for free created for us the association site, which operated as a Web portal. We could communicate with the external world with no obstacles.

My frequent visits to media began. Because the journalists got a sense, that there were gay organizations in Poland, and homosexuality was an interesting topic for them, they fell on us like vultures. Soon, my face crossed most of the existing TV stations, radio programs and newspapers. It had some good aspects, for I could show the world that a gay was not a pervert hiding from the living world, but a normal human being. Unfortunately, the thing also had the other side of the coin.

Many of my neighbors are young people. Many of them at the time were attending a high school or a college. And for most of them, it was unthinkable, that in their block of flats a gay might live. It began with invectives, then beating and attacks on my flat. When a few years later I talked to the community head of policemen, it appeared, that during three years, I was calling for the police over 200 times, once a week on average. It also happened once, that I had to extinguish fire in my flat lighted with a bottle filled with patrol thrown inside. In September 2001 someone attacked me at my working place. That was at the time, when for a short time I was working as a clerk in a fast food bar. Unfortunately, when a French owner of the bar got to know, that he employed a gay, he wanted to dismiss me. I didn't give him a satisfaction I left by myself.

During one of those attacks, an assailant took out a knife. Though, he didn't manage to stab me, for I had pepper gas on me and that frightened him away. The policemen who came to the crime scene and drove me around the neighborhood in order to find the perpetrator suggested that I should buy a gun for myself. They said that if I shoot the assailant, I would make their work easier. Though, I never decided for that move. I detest violence. Though, through all that time, when I was working in a local mall, Krzysiek was coming out to meet me with a heavy steel frying pan in a bag. That frying pan has saved our lives a couple of times.

On the 11th of September 2001 we were sitting at a meeting of the managing board of the association in the Mykonos club. We were discussing some issues related to our association and about the news of the day that day Campaign Against Homophobia (KPH) was formed, when suddenly on the TV screen switched to TVN channel, we saw an information about the terrorist attack on the World Trade Center.

We were shocked watching the collapsing buildings. At once, we decided to react, as many other people in Poland. We sent a condolence letter to the Embassy of the USA in Warsaw. A few weeks later we received warm acknowledgements. We already knew that that date changed the world.

In September 2001, bishop Tadeusz Pieronek in an interview for the Gazeta Wyborcza, make a comparison of homosexuality to a contagious disease. He stated as well, that gay couldn't be a teacher. When I suggested to Robert Biedroń, that we together, as the KPH and the ILGCN should take him to court, he said that it wouldn't make any sense. Fortunately, Joanna Sosnowska, a member of parliament from the Democratic Left Alliance, got interested in that issue and we together submitted a notice of an offence at the public persecutor's office. As you probably guess, the public persecutor's office rejected our application stating that the Polish law didn't have any obligations to protect "persons of different sexual orientation within the boundaries of their otherness." We sued that decision at the court and in this way for the first time, and hope that also the last time, I had to appear before the court. Unfortunately, the court acceded to the public persecutor's conclusion, acknowledging, that actually the Polish law didn't protect homosexual persons. A positive aspect of that case was that a woman judge reprimanded the woman public persecutor, that her justification was inapt. It was the first case, which proved that hierarchs of the Roman Catholic Church in Poland had greater laws than average citizens. We were shown, that homosexuals in Poland were people of the second category. Constitutional protection didn't transfer to the constitutional law. In practice, the situation didn't change to this day.

On the 5th of October 2001, I celebrated not only my birthday, but also the first anniversary of my relationship with Krzysiek. The TVN team got interested in our jubilee. They made a program about us as one of the first homosexual couples, which decided to show their faces. They were with us at the party. As a gift, we got two gypsum frogs painted golden, which stand in my balcony. When I watch that old TV program, I see how many people were there with us then. That was the whole range of our friends from the circle and from the outside. Today, most of them dispersed all around the world. That TV program, as well as another, "Rozmowy w Toku," in which we took part, started of a spiral of hatred toward us. Really, there were days, when it was difficult to leave home without taking a risk. We tried to leave as early as we could and come back very late, when the drunken youths were already at home. That concluded a club life. Then, we settled for good in the Sikstinajn club, where we preformed with Krzysiek.

In 2001, Ernest Ivanovs visited Poland again. This time, he didn't leave empty-handed. Together with a few friends we signed a letter of intent and we brought into existence the Initiative Group of The Free Reformed Church in Poland. Before that, I got to the Television Academy, which I graduated one year later. From the whole process of studying, I remembered the most the word of one of the lectures, who told me, that in spite of the fact that I was one of the best of his students, I didn't have a chance to get a job at the public television. There was no place there for an openly gay person.

Mum, this is my... eeer...

During all that mess, my mum was trying to keep aside. I got to know, how difficult her life was only a few years later from an interview that she gave to a women monthly Oliwia. From the moment I started to live alone, we met practically every week at a dinner at restaurants. That was a tile for free chats and exchange of gossips. In the meantime, I must admit with repentance, I was running an accelerated course of explaining the facts of life to my mum. I shared all the news from my life with her. Well, nearly all of them. About my problems with the neighbors and vandals she learned from the caretaker Ms. Krysia who lived next door, or from media. It's worth mentioning, that Ms. Krysia was a true caretaker. From the very beginning, our contacts were warm and so they are to this day. I remember, once there were a few drunken teenagers standing under my window. They cursed and swore and threw stones at the grating. Ms. Krysia dressed in her night shirt went out onto her balcony and let loose such a volley of abuse that they ran away swallowing their pride. When her younger son started to associate with my local enemies and stopped answering my greetings, I made an observation that she should talk to him, because I often called for the police and I didn't want her boy had any problems. Anyway, he never hurt me in anyway, so why he should suffer instead of other imbeciles. The following day, I saw him on my way home. He had a blacked eye and at my sight he bowed and said hello before I even came closer. I don't support family violence, but at that moment I understood, that Ms. Krystyna simply wanted her sons to grow into honest men. Today, after having lived on Sadyba for a few years, I may say, that she succeed 100%. But let's go back to my mum.

Even though, we met so often and we talked practically about everything, my mum didn't want to meet any of my partners before. She didn't feel ready for such a meeting. Though, in 2001 something cracked in her. She heard much about Krzysiek from me and she knew that I was in a real love with him and it wasn't just a passing love affair. One day, when we were driving her car back home from dinner, and made another appointment, I asked her in jest: "*Mum and when are you going to invite Krzysiek for dinner?*" I saw her hands clenching on the steering wheel and after a while, a heard her saying the words, that made me dumbfound: "*You know what? Ask him on behalf of me for the next dinner. Maybe we will go to the Bouthouse.*" At first, I couldn't believe my ears. I think that was a tough decision for her. But you had to be true to your word. A week later, me and Krzysiek dressed up in suits, kept an appointment. I really don't remember what we were having for that dinner. Admittedly, all of us were trying to pretend we were free and relaxed, but we know, how difficult that was for both parties, us and my mum. You know, that was a kind of a dinner, at which a son presents his fiancé to his mother. But the effect must have been satisfactory, for from that time, for the dinner with my mum we were coming together.

Halloween that year we spent in the Paradise club. I met there Jacek Adler and his partner, Marcin. I was dressed up as a devil, and

Krzysiek as a drag queen. Marcin was disguised as a corpse bride. We were having fun and laughing without limit. Together with Krzysiek and Marcin, we made a pretty good show on the club stage. We spent Christmas 2001 separately, yet. Krzysiek went to his family in Działdowo, I went to my mum and Adam near Warsaw. Krzysiek introduced a new tradition, every time he visited his family, he was bringing with him bags full of food. In the most difficult moments, they were saving our lives. And that happened more and more often. I could find a regular job, and Krzysiek was changing his job from time to time. And that was always accompanied by scandal. At that time, I didn't attach importance to that, but after years it occurred, that most of the things I knew about him, were only his fabrication. Thanks to that experience, I learned to verify the past of every one of my next partners. But before it came to that, we were living life of a good and loving couple, who at some point started to function in the Warsaw gay circles as an example. You had to admit, that Krzysiek was able construct his image in a perfect way. All those years we spent together, he never let anyone catch him out in a lie. I acknowledge that I was guilty as well, for I accepted all his stories as an obvious truth. My naivety was to cost me much.

In 2001 Parliament elections were held and Professor Maria Szyszkowska was elected for the Senate. She is a woman of unbending principles, a splendid philosopher and a great friend of lesbians and gays. My life and social and political activity were to be close –knit with her for long years.

Another year brought big changes. First of all, the ILGCN-Poland started to develop. There were many people interested in what we were doing. We were all looking forward to another parade, for which we started to prepare already in January.

The first spokes in our wheel...

Though, before we lived to May and the second parade, we needed to lead a life and to function. Instructed by example of the previous year, we wanted the second equality parade be prepared more professionally. To do that, we needed many allies.

Basically, just after the first parade finished, people, who would like to help us, dropped a line. That was a very edifying experience for us. We got the first real offers of help from Janusz Marchwiński and Radek Oliwa from the Inna Strona and from Sergiusz Wróblewski from the SoftPress, the publisher of the "Inaczej" magazine. Janusz and Radek were helping us in collecting funds and gathering volunteers, whereas Sergiusz helped us with the posters. That was SoftPress, who prepared for us the first project of a colorful poster of the Equality Parade. The new logo of the parade was prepared for us by the Inna Strona editorial staff. Later, that logo was found on the volunteers' T-shirts and in our leaflets. It turned out, that not everyone found our activity palatable. In March, we got a letter from the Polish branch of Minolta, which demanded from us to remove a graphic fragment from the logo of our association, which in their opinion was associated with the logo of their company. For a long time, I couldn't understand, where from Minolta could get our logo and who could make such associations, for a circle with a few stripes in the middle didn't necessarily have to be associated with that producer.

Not before 2005, during a private conversation with the publisher of the Gejowo Web portal, I learned, that Minolta was informed about the case by an "indignant client," the most probably in the person of Łukasz Pałucki – a man, who was to cause many other problems for me.

At that time, the Gejowo Web portal was at daggers drawn with us. Their editorial staff was doing everything to discredit us mostly because our main patron and a great help was their then the greatest competitor, the Inna Strona. When I look at the posters of the Equality Parade hanging on the walls of my room, I smile to myself at the recollection of those moments, when at the Gejowo I was reading libels about ILGCN and the Parade.

In spite of those combats, we managed to win the first external sponsors. As the first, the "Fakty i Mity" weekly's editorial staff had a courage to admit, that they supported the rights of homosexual persons. Those anticlerical transferred the first donation for the Equality Parade. Apart from them, officially, as sponsors in the posters was visible the Paradise club and the flapjack restaurant Bastylia. Though, thanks to a supporting action publicized by the Inna Strona, we were collecting funds till the last moment. Companies, clubs and private persons donated. We collected 3 765 zloty all together.

While the media patronage was assured by the Inna Strona, Inaczej monthly and a private Internet site Happy Together.

From preparations to the second Parade, I sadly recall problems with the organization committee. Both, the Lambda Warszawa and the Campaign Against Homophobia had already noticed a medial power of that event and decided to take advantage of that. Still in February, the talks were held and both organizations became part of the organization committee. Apart from them, Amnesty International Polska, TADA and Tolersex joined the body.

The representatives of organizations declared their help, volunteers and support... It ended only in that TADA and Tolersex put up their volunteers, who were helping us during the march. The rest of the organizations were satisfied with their logos in the posters and delegations at the Parade. Thus, again, the Equality Parade was made by 4 persons.
The 1st of May 2002 was sunny and warm.

Enjoying the help of my neighbor, a taxi driver, and a company producing balloons, we transported banners, flags and the equipment to the Nicolaus Kopernik Monument.

I must admit, that I was really surprised by the great interest of media. As opposed to the first Parade, on that day we were escorted probably by all of the existing Poland TV and radio stations. Journalists and press photographers were bustling about among us energetically. People gathered around the monument were circled by a police cordon, though at the very beginning there was nobody, we could be defended from.

We set off at 13:30. A colorful file arranged along the street and suddenly it occurred that there were around two thousand of us. I was shocked. We expected 500 persons, maybe one thousand. Whereas people instructed by experience of the previous year simply came. Admittedly, again many indecisive persons were walking down the pavement, but either way the number of the people gathered in the street was shocking. At the front the girls from the Radical Cheerleaders arranged.

Dressed in pink costumes and holding pom-poms, the girls were chanting anti-discrimination slogans. The rainbow bridge made of balloons was fluttering above their heads. The atmosphere was joyful and merry. When observing the gathered people, I spotted a few politicians in the crowd. Later, under the Zygmunt's Column, they gave a speech.

When we were passing by the gate of the Warsaw University, we encountered the activists from the All-Polish Youth for the first time. That nationalistic task force organization of a neo-fascist treated us with a slogan, which had made a history of all the Parades. "Do it at home, do it secretly" around 40 young men were chanting. They were clearly frustrated, for they didn't expect that they would be forced to face that crowd, which ridiculed and catcalled.

Under the monument of a cardinal Stefan Wyszyński, I read an appeal to the Roman Catholic Church. I entitled it "Non Possumus" – we forbid. I knew that you could elicit an adequate reaction only using a strong emphasis. And we needed a reaction. We wanted to say no to call us perverts, deviants and ill people. I got it for that appeal, but I think it was worth doing it. An interesting recollection of those events is a photo, in which the cardinal is looking thoughtfully at the rainbow hued flag billowing in front of his nose.

When we reached the Presidential Palace we were attacked by fascists from the All-Polish Youth another time. Ten youngsters started to throw eggs at us. Then, the police reacted. Immediately, they pushed them into a gate and arrested them. We awarded the police with our applause and we continued to walk. Under the Zygmunt's Column, the most colorful and moving part of the event was held.

After the speeches of the guests, we all joined our hands and we sang together the popular hit "We Are The World." I saw tears in the peoples' eyes and I myself felt a lump in my throat. After the demonstration had been finished and dismissed, we dispersed to our homes to prepare ourselves for the After Party in clubs. Of course, together with Krzysiek, we made a rush for TV and the Internet to watch and read what the world was being reported about us. And then, the first bitter feeling came. In most of the media we were either omitted or presented in a false way. False data appeared also in the gay media. Again, the Gejowo played a disgraceful role. They made fun of the whole Parade, lying by the way about the number of people who took part in it. But a real witch-hut was yet to begin.

A few days after the Parade, the Inna Strona published an article, in which they encouraged to buy a film realized during the Parade. The total profit form the sale was to go for the next Parade. And then, the Gejowo launched another attack. In their article their editorial staff accused the Inna Strona for a trial to earn money on a common idea. Taking an opportunity, they attacked also us and demanded revealing details about the finances of the Parade.

Of course, we published the financial statement, in which we accounted for every single zloty. But the Gejowo still wasn't satisfied. They couldn't pick on us for any expenditure; they invented and "discovered" a great unfair dealing that we were to commit. That was all about a bill for a mailing sent to 10 thousand persons, users of one of the tourist Web portals, for which we paid 24 zloty. According to the Gejowo, the sum of money was too little to be true. Thus, the editorial staff concluded – if we falsified such an amount, surely, our embezzlement reached thousands of zlotys.

Any reasonable person wouldn't believe those inventions but already then the first signals occurred, that in the homosexual society, a division into followers and opponents of gay organizations and their leaders. The next "shocking discoveries" of the Gejowo editorial staff were to emerge soon.

Though before it came to another scandal me and Krzysiek decided to raise a subject of culture. Thus, the ILCGN-Poland announced their first all-Poland literary contest with the subject matter of homosexuality. The award of the Rainbow Pen was so inviting, that over 30 persons applied for the first edition. Among others, Professor Maria Szyszkowska, a laureate of the Rainbow Laurels, sat on the jury. At that time she performed a function of a Senator of the Polish Republic. Thanks to her support, we managed to implement a project of the contest, to buy awards and to present them in a suitable binding. On the 2nd of October 2002, Ms. Professor received the title of a Honorary Member of our association, at the same time becoming the first Polish parliamentarian – a member of the homosexual organization.

In August, in a tragic car accident, Marek Kotański, died. He was a man of a great heart, a protector of homeless, drug addicts and other persons excluded from the society. At his funeral, I represented homosexual society. That fact evoked an ascertainment among the clergy assembled. Some people clearly didn't like my words, saying that Marek cuddled to his heart everyone including gays and lesbians. I was standing in the rain in the Warsaw Powązki cemetery, and I was telling: "*In the reality surrounding us, there are many people, for whom the only value is money and fame. Also, there many people, who would like to eliminate from their surroundings everything and everyone, who are different from what they regard as normal. Luckily, there are also many people, who with all their might contradict a growing wave of hatred and intolerance – people, for whom tolerance and acceptance are the highest values. Marek Kotański always sided with us, people oppressed, referred to as the dregs of society. He gave us support and helped us at the moments, when nobody wanted to deal with a problem of homosexuality, which was embarrassing for the Polish authorities. He never rejected anyone only because she or he was a lesbian or a gay. In the world of today, deprived of the basic human values, it's very much. We rewarded him with the highest decoration, which the Polish homosexual persons may award. But the award of the Rainbow Laurels is only a drop in the bucket of our thankfulness. He was a friend to all of us. Calling them, you could always be sure, that he would the find time to answer even the most difficult questions and he would help you to get rid of any bothering doubts. It is the more painful for us, cause we wouldn't have a chance to tell Marek, how much grateful we are to him. For today, when we say goodbye to You, Marek, we can tell you only one thing: Thank you! Thank you, that you were one of not many people, who had courage to be a friend of all homosexual people. Thank you... And see you. See you, for the people, like you never die. They live for ever in the hearts and minds of those, in which they managed to, instill their love of another person."* That was one of my first public speeches, at which I directly met the politicians of Poland and persons in authority.

In 2002, other local elections were held. Also at that time, for the first time I associated with the Anticlerical Progress Party RACJA, which asked me to stand from their list for the elections for the Warsaw Town Council. I agreed and started to seriously prepare for the elections, when on the day of the final registration, it turned out, that my name was removed from the list without explanation. Quite a big scandal came out of that and I resigned from politics for a dozen or so months. Only the events of the year 2003 made me come back to the political stage with the election of Lech Kaczyński as Mayor of Warsaw.

I was working hard as a social worker. Together with ILGCN, we were reacting to all the cases of homophobia in the public life. We had the courage to submit a notice of an offence committed by Bishop Tedeusz Pieronek at the public persecutor's office. In an interview for Gazeta Wyborcza, Pieronek stated, that homosexuality was a contagious disease. Unfortunately, that gave no results, because the court stated that the Polish law didn't protect homosexual persons in either way.

We were cooperating with the Office of the Commissioner of Equal Status of Women and Men. There I met Izabella Jaruga Nowacka and her collaborator, Katarzyna Kądziela.

At the same time, I decided to continue my education and I signed up for the Television Academy. That was a postgraduate college ran with the cooperation of my first college that was the College of Communication and Social Media. From my year-long studies at the Academy, two situations fixed in my mind. The first was still during my studies, when Stanisław Pieniak, a friend of my father and a lecturer at the TA, told me that in spite of my favorable conditions and good professional education, I didn't have a chance to get a job at the public television as an openly gay person. The other, even more nasty situation, happened at the defense my thesis, when Ms. Katarzyna Korpolewska, a psychologist running the college, stated that she was very sorry, that her best student became a gay. I felt insulted to that extent that I decided not to take my diploma. I suppose that it's lying in the deanery of the CCSM still.

On the 5th October me and Krzysiek were celebrating the first anniversary of my relationship. Because, by accident, the SuperWizjer's TVN team, wanted to make a program about us, we invited them to our little party. I must admit, that it was very nice of a woman journalist to give us at the beginning two huge gypsum frogs painted golden. They've stood in my balcony to this day and remind me of the old, good times. The program itself wasn't really good and provoked many controversies, mainly because the host tried to suggest, that we demanded rights for adoption of children by homosexual couples.

Our cooperation with Polsat TV and journalist Zakrzewski finished with a similar effect. Zakrzewski tormented us for nearly two days making the program "Homosexuality in Polish." In spite of his great wish to show both striptease and drag queens, thanks to help of Professor Maria Szyszkowska, we managed to fight out some changes and take part in the editing and acceptance of the material. Thanks to that, the program worked out quite good.

We began to have more and more such adventures with TV cameras. Together with Krzysiek, we had taken part in over 40 TV programs. I stopped counting the interviews given to the press and radio after the first one hundred.

In 2002 I already had long hair, which in a way became my symbol. The circles started to divide into supporters of short-haired Robert Biedroń and long-haired Szymon Niemiec. For a few following years, on Web portals and in newspapers a discussion on the topic, if a long-haired man could represent interests of homosexual persons.

I cut my hair a bit at the end of 2002, when I started to have problems with split ends. Besides, I ended my cooperation with the photographic agency and further growing of long hair wasn't necessary.

One day in August I met Robert Biedroń at the occasion of discussing some questions. At those times, we used to meet quite often in clubs and equally often we used to talk about various issues related to ways of operating in our community. I remember, that I was still thinking about a question asked by one of the journalists, who wanted to know, how you could lead to a situation, in which the Polish society would get to know lesbians and gays as normal people. Then, we already knew, that alone parades wouldn't solve the problem. While talking to Robert, I asked him, what was his opinion was of organizing a photo exhibition of normal lesbians and gays. After a short discussion, Robert said, that such an exhibition would never succeed. Firstly, we wouldn't find people with courage to show their faces. And secondly, such an exhibition would be a great expense and nobody would give us the money for that. I agreed with him, knowing the reality of our activity, and I put the idea aside. Imagine my surprise, when a few weeks later, KPH proudly announced the beginning of a project "Let Them See Us," an exhibition of photographs of homosexual couples in everyday situations and usual poses. I thought o myself, that probably Robert Biedron had thought the thing over and decided to employ my idea. Though, I was surprised, why he asked Lambda to cooperate forgetting about ILGCN. Though, when Katarzyna Breguła, a photographer, who undertook making to photos for that project, turned to me, I didn't refuse. Together with Krzysiek, we posed for the photographs.

The project moved full speed ahead and the production lasted for the next seven months. Ultimately, the first vernissage was held in June the following year. Of course, it didn't go without scandals with participation of the League of Polish Families and advertising agencies, which were doing everything not to allow the billboards and posters advertising the action. I still have nice memories of the event itself, though I remember a stab of sorrow, when I saw a picture of me thrust in the corner of the gallery and Robert Biedron, who boasted in front of the cameras telling the journalists about his struggle for the exhibition.

At the same time, a senator, Ms. Maria Szyszkowska, turned to me for help. It occurred; that she had began working on a bill on registration of free relationships. She asked me for consultations on that matter. The first, initial projects were very radical and they didn't give us a chance for acceptance in the Sejm. After thorough and lasting for many months' works, they managed to construct a project suitable to present to the public opinion. Many various circles and organizations took part in the works over the bill, though many of them treated the bill with the tongue in their cheek. Meanwhile, new persons started to join our association. Jacek Adler and Marcin Mich, a couple, which I had met a little earlier, entered the association. Fate connected me with them for many years in a strange relation that was swinging from friendship to hatred and back again. Before that, they had experienced a membership in the KPH, but soon they ended cooperation with Robert Biedroń. Both gentlemen remained in the ILGCN for a short term and their stay ended with the biggest possible scandal.

I don't remember exactly, why Jacek and Marcin were removed from the association, and how the matter of a false earning certificate of Marcin ensued. Anyway, the whole thing took a quick course and at a closed-circuit joined meeting of the managing board and audit committee, both men were suspended in the association membership rights. I thought that the whole thing would be over with that, and we could continue our work in peace. But I didn't take into account Jacek's revengeful nature and, what's even worse, the lust for sensation of the Gejowo's publisher.

Soon after that event, Jacek Adler became an editor-in-chief of the Gejowo. That information didn't stir me, but already at the beginning of the year 2003, I was to learn, what Jacek was capable of doing.

Who, of whom, for what and for how much...

A few days after Jacek had been appointed the editor-in-chief of the Gejowo, on a Web portal a text appeared signed by a "nemesis." I learned about that fact thanks to the people I knew and journalists, who flooded me with e-mails and telephones. Everyone was asking me, if that's true, that I was a thief charged by the public persecutor's office for embezzlement and fraudulent alteration of documents. I was shocked. When I entered the Gejowo, the first thing that caught my eye was a photo of me and Krzysiek with black stripes across our eyes and a big headline: "Szymon N. and Krzysztof Sz. Charged At The Persecutor's Office."

The author gave oneself much trouble to paint everything that related to our private lives in black colors. Some of the allegations were so absurd, that even the readers, who commented on them, were tapping their forehead. To me, the most amusing was an accusation, that as private person, I started a business activity in order to organize cabaret shows. He didn't give himself enough trouble to learn, what kind of business activity in a democratic country was an offence, but he thundered forth about that through the whole paragraph. Another "crashing" proof of my guilt was to be a fact that I took up a credit as a private person. Nemesis depicted me as an alcoholic, who was drinking away the ILGCN money at the parties organized at my flat. That was insomuch funny, that the ILGCN had never had any cash, which could be embezzled. Most of the income, which were carefully documented and published on the Internet site of the association once a year, came from our private purses.

The heaviest reproach, which I was to face, was a slander of a fraudulent alteration of documents. The Gejowo even published a scan of a document issued by me and confirming that I employed Marcin Mich. Together with Krzysiek, we made a decision to submit a notice of an offence at the public persecutor's office immediately. At the same time, I started to look for a lawyer, who would conduct a court action for libel against the Gejowo. All in all, I visited maybe 8 law firms, in which the lawyers were willing to take up our case, because on the basis of the documents, they knew beforehand it would be won. Unfortunately, every one of them demanded a fee of over 5 thousand zloty. And we just couldn't afford such expenditures.

A few days after the whole scandal erupted, two Web portals turned to us. The Inna Strona asked me for an interview and a comment, while the Homo.pl decided to unravel the whole thing on the way of a journalist investigation.

In the interview for the IS I told my version of the events and described the whole intrigue, in which Jacek Adler was trying to get me mixed up. I lavished bitter words aimed at him and the Gejowo. Of course, I was aware, that it wouldn't be easy to make for the wrong they did. At once, the society had divided into those, who believed in that absolute rubbish and those, who didn't believe it. Those first ones weren't convinced even by the article on the Homo.pl, which author was the only person, who took the trouble and asked us for an insight into the financial documents of the association and of my private finances, and then he published a dependable report, which conclusion was lack of any proof of committing crime by me.

The public persecutor's office refused to institute legal proceedings against me after Jacek has submitted a notice of an offence in order to get his revenge for our notice against him. The reason for the refusal was the lack of special features of committing a prohibited act. After a conversation with the persecutor, I fell to his persuasion and I withdrew my motion to persecute Jacek and Marcin. I was convincing then, that the scandal would finally die away. Unfortunately, it occurred that there are people, who take that libel against me even today. The Gejowo, in spite of my repeated demands, has never removed the text from their archives. Maybe someday they would finally remove it, because, as the editor himself admits, at present, the text does more harm to them, than to me.

But before that, that text from the Gejowo, was used by a few right wing and catholic Web portals, as a proof for their stipulation, that homosexual society was bad and spoiled to the marrow. Today, when I'm looking back, I can see that in some cases those homophobic articles were right. Indeed, in our Polish society there exists some peculiar manner to destroy everything that is good. Everyone, who will go further above mediocrity, has to count with the fact, that there will be people for whom pushing you back into the morass of vagueness will be the greatest goal. Anyway, this applies not only to gays, but generally to the whole of the Polish society.

In 2003 a clear division into three groups within the homosexual society began. The first one was a group of the "children of the clubs." The group consisted mainly of the people under 25 year old, for whom indeed being a gay or a lesbian was limited exclusively to the live in a closed world of clubs, parties and discos. They were not interested in any kind of activity, or any rights, except having fun. Their world was filled with music, lights and new clothes. Reaching them with any offer of cooperation was equal to a miracle. We had to learn to take advantage of their love of clubbing through organizing commercial events, the profit from which supported the treasury of the association.

The most engaged in social and political activity group were so called "children of the Internet." Regardless of the fact, that their world was still a virtual space, it was that group, who showed the greatest motivation for activity. Of course, also among those people there were many malcontents, eternal grumblers or destroyers, but most of the Internet society showed a greater social and political awareness from the rest of the homosexual persons. It was on the Internet, that new ideas and concepts were born, understanding was initiated, and support groups were born – sometimes transforming into groups of mutual adoration. The third and the most numerous group functioning in the homosexual society was a group of the "closet." People, who belonged to it, were characterized by living in hiding.

Nobody knew about their existence, often even the environs. They were the people, who like fire dread any contacts with so called community, for which they regarded to be the members of the two previous groups I discussed. They displayed their presence with help of the Web portals directed to the whole Polish society, through writing comments under articles, through the letters, telephone calls and e-mails sent to the homosexual organizations.

Their activity focused mainly either on remonstrating with the lifestyle of other homosexual people and with activity of the LGBT leaders or on a desperate looking for help. At the beginning of my social work, I used to archive every letter, a telephone call or an e-mail. When their number exceeded a few thousand I ceased this kind of activity. Simply, there was no sense in it. My mobile used to experience a real siege, especially at nights, when an official help line of the Lambda Warsaw didn't work. Then, desperate parents of homosexual persons were calling, as well as lesbians and gays themselves, who were looking for help.

In April 2003, the preparations for the Equality Parade were already very advanced. Also then, for the first time we managed to convince all the organizations to cooperate with us actively. Both, the Lambda Warsaw and the Campaign Against Homophobia already understood, that the Parade was a perfect moment for presentation their organizations and not taking advantage of that chance would be a manifestation of stupidity. The two organizations, as usual, the Society of the Young and Free Tolersex, and for the first time, a women organization Fest sQad, applied to us with an offer of help. The program was so well promising, that we decided to stagger it into 3 days, in this way creating the Culture Days Queer.

During a private conversation in the office of Ms. Szyszkowska a Polish Senator, a proposal was put forward to her, if she would like to take the Parade under her auspices. Professor Szyszkowska agreed and the Equality Parade gained its first official patron. The second patron was Euro-parliamentarian, Joke Swiebel. The three days of the may long weekend were closely filled with a cultural, social and political program. Medial patronage was assured by all the gay and lesbian Web portals in Poland, with a disgraceful exception in the form of the Gejowo. As well, the list of sponsors was already significantly long, though most of them didn't donate the money, but either helped in collecting the funds or funded some kind of additional items for the Parade.

We expected a big attendance and instructed by experience from previous years we decided to hire a platform with the PA system installed. A week before the Parade, revolutionary information reached us that the second platform for the Parade was being prepared by the Szczecin chapter of the Self-Defense of the Republic of Poland. We even heard that Andrzej Lepper and other prominent politicians of the Self-Defense were to appear at the Parade. Ultimately, it didn't come to their presence, but a platform sponsored by one of the clubs from Szczecin and the youth association attached to the Self-Defense's, constituted a very interesting element of the Parade. The Inna Strona, which, as every year, took the medial patronage of the Parade, described that event as the biggest Polish demonstration. The following text is their assessment of the event: "*Over three and a half thousand of people marched through the streets of Warsaw in the third, and the biggest as for the moment the Equality Parade. This year rainbow feast was a great organizational success of the International Lesbian & Gay Culture Network. One of the radio stations informed us, that the Parade was the biggest demonstration of the 1st of May in the capital city. The route led from the Castle Square, through the Krakowskie Przedmieście and Nowy Świat to the Sejm building, where the final demonstration was held. An appeal to the authorities of the Polish Republic was read by the president of the ILGCN, Szymon Niemiec. On the behalf of the Sejm, the appeal was received by a vice president of the Chancellery of the Sejm. As well, a member of the European Parliament, Joke Swiebel, and the chief of the Federation of the Women' Rights, Wanda Nowicka, who were present at the Parade, gave a speech. In spite of declarations, none of the politicians allegedly supporting sexual minorities appeared. The march set off at 13:30 sharp. Its head was a decorated platform with the sound equipment. Behind it, the groups with banners of various organizations followed: ILGCN, KPH, Tolersex, the Greens and many others. The column, which occupied one line of the road, was a few hundred meters long. Behind it, a huge platform from Szczecin followed, on which popular drag queenies were dancing to the sound of music and in company of a singer, Krystyna Prońko. There were also funny elements. Just before the march out, the police securing the demonstration "arrested" a drag queen Daruma, who was dressed up as a police woman. After they took away from her the "official uniform insignia," she could continue her travel together with the other disguised people in a white American limo.*

There were no records of any perturbations. Only in the vicinity of the Plac Trzech Krzyży a group of a few youngsters from the fascist All-Polish Youth gathered. Their pathetic provocation was quickly ended by the police. The crowds of passersby on the pavements were looking at the rainbow parade with interest. Many people were taking photos or reading the distributed leaflets. Also on the pavements, every now and again you could see gay couples, who clearly didn't have enough courage to join the march. Maybe next year?

As Szymon Niemiec informed us, the permit for the Parade was given by the President of Warsaw, Lech Kaczyński in person. He did it at the last moment, after having heard the opinions of all the public services engaged. Because there was no basis for a refusal to the permit for the demonstration, he had to put his signature to it. In the evening, in the Warsaw clubs parties and entertainments began, which attracted throngs of gays and lesbians who coming from the whole Poland."

Actually, the paradox of the event, which I've been stressing for the following years, was the fact, that the president of the capital city, Lech Kaczyński in person, gave the permit for the Parade. His swearing in the following years, that he had never given such a permit was a notorious lie, besides, not the first and not the last.

**I cannot give permission for gay parade.
I don't have good costume**

Ernest Ivanovs also appeared at the Parade. This time, he was going with us officially in his liturgical vestments. A few persons came up to him and asked why he dressed himself up as a priest. When they got to know, that he was a pastor, they congratulated him for his courage. He was also congratulated for the same courage by few Catholic priests, who were taking part in the Parade incognito. After the Parade, Ernest decided to move to Poland in order to establish the Free Reformed Church in our country. We started to meet in the Le Madame club founded by Krystian Legierski, and then still an assistant of professor Szyszkowska. In the basement of the club, in a room, this resembled some mediaeval crypt, our religious group used to meet. There weren't many of us, but we felt really united. With time, also heterosexual persons started to attend our divine services. Ernest had a unique gift of winning the favor of people. Unfortunately, he also attracted people who desired to abuse him. At that, he was very similar to me. He was to pay with a high price for that naïve trust. I think that I was the person, who understood his embitterment, like no one else, when in 2005 he had to leave Poland and return to Latvia.

When the memories of the Parade faded, we came back to our everyday business and duties. Our working over our legislative proposal had drew to a close and together with professor Szyszkowska we started to deliberate, how to introduce it at the session of the Parliament. In the meetings in her senatorial office, all the gay organizations and representatives of the Web portals met. I remember, that already then you could sense a certain distance on the part of KPH. At one of the last meetings, the representatives of the Campaign and Lambda were missing. I was at the meeting with Krzysiek and there were also a few persons from outside of the community.

When we were discussing possible ways of putting a strain on the politicians, I hit up on an idea to reach for help of the public opinion. Our aim was to collect the highest possible number of signatures under a letter of support for the bill. Ms. Szyszkowska liked the idea and in the end of July 2003, we and our friends took to collecting signatures throughout Poland. I was very surprised by the fact, that KPH joined our action very unwillingly. To be honest, except a declaration, which was informing that the bill was worked out with cooperation of the lawyers of the organization and thanks to that the project had a support of that organization, there were no real activities of the KPH. Meanwhile, the action of collecting the signatures was dynamically developing.

In most of the clubs the boxes of the ILGCN were put, in which you could drop filled and signed letters of support. Also, a wide flow of letters came in also via Internet. Though, the Democratic Left Alliance still took the unbending position that it wasn't worth mentioning.

Not before the moment, when the parliamentary club had received a pile of signed documents from us, and professor Szyszkowska, thanks to her pertinacity, led to a sitting of the club and a discussion over the bill, the authorities of the Alliance started to soften.

In spite of the fact, that in the previous elections, the Democratic Left Alliance mentioned about the fight for the minority rights in their electoral platform, the authorities of that party were doing everything not to let the bill see the light of day. They evaded as they could, but at some point they couldn't evade us and the public opinion any longer. The issue entered at a session of the parliamentary club and after a ling and stormy debate, it was decided that is would be passed on to the Senate Speaker. I honestly admit, that the thing which memorized the best from the whole debate, was a grimace on the Oleksy's, a member of the parliament, face, when he was ironically asking, who needs such a bill, cause nobody knew, how many homosexuals were voting for the SLD. Then, I told him, that we knew, because we made such a research. When I presented him the results of the questionnaires, from which it followed, that 60% of the community was voting for the SLD, he looked very confused and he never mentioned that matter again.

Nevertheless, the commotion produced an effect. The Democratic Left Alliance decided to introduce the bill at the parliament sitting, giving it support. But before it came to that, another political party revealed itself, which decided to support our initiative. That party appeared to be the Anticlerical Progress Party RACJA.

An anticlerical Christian... What else?

When we sent information to media, that we were collecting signatures for a bill, a weekly "Fakty i Mity" turned to us and offered us a free advertising and publishing of a letter, under which, the readers of the FiM could collect signatures. Meanwhile, we were observing with regret, that all the parties, which during the elections had declared a support for our demands, stayed totally silent. And then, my telephone rang.

In the receiver, I heard Piotr Musiał's voice, a chairman of the APP RACJA. He asked me, if we could meet. Remembering my so far bad experience with the party, I agreed to meet exceptionally unwillingly. I doubted, it was worth to meet the people, who had already made a fool of me once. Though, this time, my inborn inclination to forgiving, was to bring positive results.

We made an appointment to meet in one of the Warsaw cafés. When I saw a young man in a suit, which seeing me he stood up and extended his hand in my direction, I was surprised, for I didn't suspect that the chief of the party was someone so young. Piotr greeted me and when we both installed in the armchairs, he made me speechless with just one sentence.

We were to meet in the matter of support of the bill concerning registration of partner relationships, whereas he started our conversation with apologies. He stated, that the way his party treated me in the local authorities elections, was a total mistake and lack of respect. Then he added that he realized that after such an experience anyone probably wouldn't like to have anything to do with his people. In spite of that fact, he wanted to meet me and apologize and then discuss the ways, in which his party could help in our matter. I honestly confess that I was endeared immediately. I appreciated in people their ability to admit their mistake, apologizing and a trial to rectify. Piotr is a quintessence of such an attitude towards life.

Our first meeting of necessity didn't long last, but we managed to touch on many issues. There occurred a casual question that in Poland there were not a single politician, who was openly gay. Piort confirmed the RACJA's will to support our bill and we made another appointment to meet. It came to that a few weeks later. The RACJA was already collecting signatures and media informed with astonishment, that that little and controversial party was the first one which officially supported a bill giving the same-sex couples the rights similar to the rights of the heterosexual couples. Anyway, as a result, the remaining left wing parties woke up and, with greater or lesser enthusiasm, gave the bill support. Finally, the SLD came to a conclusion, that they couldn't remain silent and they officially supported the bill and that they directed that for the social consultation and for the parliamentary course.

At another meeting with Piotr, I called his attention to the fact, that his political party was poorly visible in media because except the "Fakty i Mity," it practically didn't show up anywhere. Piotr accepted my argument and we started to discuss the causes of that state of being. It occurred that the party didn't have anybody, who would see to creating its media image. There wasn't either a spokesperson or a PR Manager. After a short while, Piotr asked me, if I wouldn't like to take the duties. I asked for a few days to think it over and after having consulted the matter with professor

Szyszkowska and my own family, I said yes. When I asked Piotr, if he wasn't afraid to entrust the function of the spokesperson to an openly gay person, he shrugged his shoulders and said: *"Is it my business, with whom you sleep? The others shouldn't care about it either."* And in his way, I became the first public gay in Poland, who was in charge of an important function in a political party.

Immediately after the Party Management and the National Council had approved my nomination, we called a press conference, at which we informed about that event. Congratulations from friends and acquaintances started to pour in. There were also some remarkably unhappy persons.

Troubled Robert Biedroń, having forgotten for the moment, that he himself belonged to the SLD, was telling about unnecessary politicizing of the LGBT movement and unnecessary binding with such a controversial party.

Some people from the community accused me that binding with the APP RACJA; I was making fool of myself and the LGBT movement. Though, I noticed, that media, which so far treated me as a phenomenon from the borderland of a social absurd, started to approach me very seriously. They started to ask me about issues concerning my philosophy of life, a pacifist movement and the individual's rights. The topic of homosexuality ceased to play the main role. I proved that you could be a gay and at the same time have political and social, or economical views. That was a big shock for people, who were convinced, that the small handful of homosexuals was interested exclusively in sex and nothing more.

The following country councils and the party meetings were a great occasion for me to meet my women and men colleagues from the party. Slowly, with a big support from Piotr, I managed to convince even those the most hardened, that anticlericalism wasn't everything. The APP RACJA began to appear at the anti-war demonstrations, feminist demonstrations and marches. We started to be noticed also thanks to a successive reminding media about our presence. That consisted in a hard work, in looking for topics and constructing press notes, which had to be sent very frequently. At some point, our press conferences started to produce an effect and the APP RACJA started to appear in the newspapers as a full political being. Thanks to cooperation with professor Szyszkowska, we were invited for scientific and political conferences, and the science people ceased to look at us as if we were a gang of fanatics fighting with the Church. For me it was a period of strenuous work. Every telephone call from the senatorial office had such an effect, that me and Krzysiek were leaving everything and dashed to the other end of Warsaw to bring something, to help with something or to attend to some matters. At some moment, I started to be treated on the office nearly as a member of the household. We were often discussing many various subjects, and we were frequently of different opinions, but we always came to common conclusions.

Up to that moment, I didn't have anything to do with transsexual, and I didn't realize how difficult the life of the people who were transsexual was. But when in the association, a transsexual person appeared, her problem made me decide to engage in the issue closer. Thanks to cooperation with professor Szyszkowska we organized a meeting of such persons. Not many of them came; nevertheless, the multitude of their problems was shocking. In Poland we were at the stage of noticing homosexual persons. Nobody was talking about transsexuals. The transsexual persons themselves weren't ready for outing. We were trying to persuade them to present themselves at a scientific conference, it ended in that, and I had to read out the letter in front of the audience on their behalf. That was a good trick for media, because it called attention to the fact that those persons existed actually outside the political discourse. A short time later, in the Lambda Warsaw, a support group for the transsexual persons arose. I received that with joy.

Meanwhile, in my private life many things were happening. One day, an unknown to me women called me and she stated, that she had to meet me in a matter concerning my father. At that time, I had already survived a few assassination attempts, so I agreed to a meeting, but we made an appointment in the Sikstinajn bar, where not only everybody knew me, but where I could feel safe. Before the meeting, I asked the bartenders for discrete protection.

When I arrived at the meeting, in the garden of the bar, an older woman was waiting for me. The first thing she did, was asking me if she could see my hands. The woman examined my little finger of my right hand very thoroughly, which is a little bit distorted from birth. Suddenly, in her eyes filled with tears. She asked me if I knew that I had a brother. I was totally shocked. I didn't know, what I should say, while Zosia – because that was her name – started to tell me, that she was mother of my half-sibling brother, 4 years younger than me. At first, I didn't want to believe her, but when she showed me a picture of her son, I recognized in him our common family features. Zosia managed to convince me, that I had a brother, whose name was Krzysztof, who had been looking for me for years, but my father was doing everything not to let us meet. She told me so many details from the life of my father and his partner, that she just wouldn't be able to invent that. She suggested that I should meet Krzysiek. I was so much shocked, that I asked her for a few days to consider the offer.

Right away, when I got home, I wrote an e-mail to my father asking him for an explanation. I received an answer, on which my father claimed, that that woman wanted to destroy him and Krzysiek wasn't my brother, but just a cousin, besides, and after all, my mother knew him. And what's more, Krzysiek was a homophobe, and he hated me for being a gay. Besides, he didn't have to excuse himself to me from his life. I felt crushed, because I realized I was being cheated all my life.
At once, I phoned mum and asked her for an urgent meeting the next day. I explained her on the telephone that the matter was related to father and it couldn't be cleared in any other way, than during a meeting face to face. We met in a café. I showed her the letter asking her for taking an attitude towards its content. Mum flied into a rage. She said, that she presumed, that father could have some more children, but she didn't suspect, that he cheated on her 4 years after they married. The

same day in the evening my younger brother called me.

I didn't know then, how much of the letter was the truth and how much was a lie. I was afraid of that meeting. My partner wanted to go with me, but I knew that for the first meeting I should meet my brother face to face. We made an appointment for the next day. Having in memory a picture, in which Krzysiek looked like a short well built and shaved to the zero boy, I came to the club an hour before the time and I asked the club staff to save my skin in case anything happened. After all, I didn't know, if he really wasn't a homophobe and if he wouldn't like to beat me. It seemed to me, I was waiting the whole eternity. At some moment, I saw him going in my direction. I stood up and extended my hand to greet him.

I expected, that we would say hello and start talking. Whereas Krzysiek fell into my arms and he just started to weep. Probably, I don't have to tell you, that I fell apart straight away. We were standing there for a few minutes and weeping like babies, while the club staff gathered around us was wiping tears discretely. That scene, like from a cheap melodrama, would be even funny, if not the fact, that it was happening in real life. We spent a few hours in the Sikstinajn telling one another in turn about everything.

At some moment, I noticed it was already late and I had to come back home. I invited him to come together with me. Krzysiek consented and in this way he met my partner.

Later, me and my Krzysiek were visiting my brother and Zosia for dinners. Also, at that time, I decided to break my contacts with father entirely. I couldn't forgive him that he took away from me my brother, who I always wanted to have.

My brother appeared to be a wonderful man. He was a student of philosophy endowed with uncommon manual talents, who could charm out real wonders with his crayons. When he got from me a set of crayons as a Christmas gift, he repaid me with a picture, which is today hanging on my wall. He is keen on tattoo and modern music. He composes and writes lyrics to hip hop songs. Every day, I was more and more proud of him. Though, we are not in such a close contact, as we were then, he is still someone very important in my life.

Blindfold torn off...

At our home, it wasn't good in 2003. Krzysiek was loosing jobs one by one, we had big financial problems and in addition, my partner started to complain about various health problems. At that point, I should have recalled my story with Pacco, but then I just couldn't believe that someone, with whom I lived for so many years, could deceive me.

One day, Krzysiek fainted at home and I couldn't bring him back to senses, so I called for an ambulance. They took him to a hospital at Banacha Street. I went with him, but they didn't let me enter the ward. For the next few days, nobody wanted to inform me, if he was alive and what happened to him.

Finally, after nearly a week, they let me in to see him and I could learn that everything was all right. It was getting worse and worse between us. I was taking successive credits, which went mainly on repayment of my previous debts. Actually, at some point I was the only person, who was bringing the money home. Krzysiek claimed, that he worked as an assistant in the Warsaw School of Economics and he often disappeared from home to give lectures, as he maintained.

He was telling me about those lectures so suggestively, that nobody even thought about checking on him. Though, when he didn't invite me for the defense of his master title, I started to have some doubts.

At the end of the year, I was so much frustrated with the whole thing, that every now and then we had dustups. My mum, who was updated on what was going on, was trying to mitigate the situation. Though, even she didn't know the seriousness of the situation. Krzysiek confessed to me, that he has another, old debt amounting to 10 thousand zlotys and all the money from the Warsaw School of Economics went for its repayment. I was close to despair. When in December, a bailiff looking for Krzysiek appeared in our door, the cup of bitterness ran over. The bailiff showed me documents, from which it followed, that Krzysiek owed private people and institutions much over 100 thousand zlotys. That damped my spirits. When in addition, the bailiff informed me, that Krzysiek was in arrears with repayment of the credit, that he took already during our relationship and he didn't tell me about it, something broke inside me. I asked him to move out of my flat as quickly as possible. We sat together and added up our common covenants and divided it evenly. I was to repay his loan in the

Provident, while he in exchange was to repay our common obligations towards our acquaintances. When moving out, he took away a beautiful steel bed, which we bought together, my television set and a video cassette player. I was left with debts. Besides, Krzysiek effectively managed to alienate me from the most of our common acquaintances. A few months later, I got to know, how perfidious methods he employed to convince everyone round us what a monster I was. A few years later, one of our friends showed me a letter, in which Krzysiek accused me of cheating on him. What's more, he was trying to involve my mum and my grandma in all that. Unraveling of some of those "revelations" took me many months.

Soon after he moved out, I started to collect the mail and registered letters for myself. It turned out, that most of them were summons to a payment directed to Krzysiek. When a vindicatory company, which haunted him, asked, where they could find him, I referred them to the Warsaw School of Economics, where he was to work. One of the workers of that company called me again later and informed me, that at the WSE nobody heard about Mr. Szymborski. Then, we mustered with a group of friends and started to search. The effects of our investigation totally frightened me.

All our common life occurred to be one big intrigue made by Krzysiek. All information, that we had checked, revealed one by one the dark inner history of his life. A doctorate that he boasted of in public appeared to be a lie, just as his two master titles. There was no offer of going to China, on which we had lived for a few months.

There were no lucrative contracts or publishing proposals. Finally, I had to face the truth. I was being deceived all those years. I let him make a fool of me and, what's even worse; I supported him in many things with my name.

If not my mum, who was patiently helping me to get out of depression, I would have never collected myself.

The New Years Eve 2003/2004 I spent in a circle of new acquaintances. I was trying to forget about all the humiliations. In the community I was still associated with Krzysiek and every now and then I had to face the questions of the kind: "How is Krzysiek?" That was a real horror for me. Though, luckily, with time, the affair grew quiet and Krzysiek disappeared from our life. He was slowly loosing friends one by one, when the truth reached them. Finally, I stopped hearing about him. The thing was ultimately closed with a decision of the town council, by virtue of which he was stroke off the list of the people registered in Warsaw. I hope that I would never hear about him again.

After the parting, I had to tend to the issues of the association myself. Luckily, the newly elected managing board helped me to find an accountant office and to clear the financial issues. My private life was overwhelmed by chaos and in spite of a few transient relationships; I couldn't find that person, with whom I could unite my fate. I was surrounded by odium of an activist and a public person, and what followed, in my surroundings appeared individuals, who either wanted to take advantage of the fact of my company or they couldn't found themselves in a situation of being with someone recognizable. It wasn't easy, but I still believed, that soon everything would shape well.

Political life in Poland started to get colored. A few new political parties arose. A referendum concerning access to EU, which was to be held soon, a big number of debates, conferences and meetings didn't let me be worried about my private affairs for too long.

The moment of founding the Green Party 2004 in Warsaw is worth mentioning. It was created by a group of passionate ecologists, feminists and social activists. I was impressed by their ideas and enthusiasm with which they got down to work. Though, my zeal cooled immediately, when I got to know that among them was Łukasz Pałucki, one of the editors of the Gejowo Web portal and a man, who let himself be known as a person completely unworthy of trust. Together with him, also Jacek Adler joined the first make-up of the Greens. Then, he was still an editor-in-chief of the Gejowo. For me, that was a serious warning signal. Both men created within the Greens a circle called Grove/Coppice, which was a group, which was to deal with an activity for the homosexual persons. At the same time, the Greens got engaged strongly in promoting the idea of the access of Poland to the European Union. One of their promotional actions was hanging the posters showing Jacek Adler tenderly embracing with Marcin and a slogan saying: "To EU for changes."

The career of Jacek and Łukasz in the Greens' party didn't last long. The members of the Warsaw circle quickly found out, that the two gentlemen cared more for promoting themselves than for a real activity and finally they thanked them for cooperation and said good-bye. Jacek after a row with the publisher of the Gejowo, left the Web portal. While

Łukasz engaged himself into creating a LGBT Foundation. The Foundation was arising in an absolute secret, but the moment of its public presentation was a truly great event.

For their program board, they invited such notabilities, as a doctor Jacek Kochanowski and professor Maria Szyszkowska. Both of those persons didn't realize, in what intrigue they let themselves be involved. Unfortunately, already then Łukasz Pałucki was famous for that he wasn't able to do without intrigues and unconsidered actions. The first and the last scandal, which ultimately compromised the idea of the foundation, was a famous speech of Łukasz to the media, in which he informed, that one of the goals of the foundation was to lead to a forced outing of the right wing politicians, who were hostile towards homosexuals. That declaration triggered off a real storm in the media. The journalists were asking us, why destroy people's lives and what kind of proof did they have. I had been long, before Robert Biedroń, Yga Kostrzewa managed to explain, that absurd idea was not a postulate of the community, but only an ill-considered extravagance of Pałucki. Nevertheless, that event seriously embittered the political situation.

When I look at the idea of forced outing, I silently laugh, for if Pałucki hadn't told that in public, and if he turned even to me, or to the PinkPress and if he asked for help, such an action might have been conducted more peacefully, and with strong proof. Because already then, in the community functioned some information about some right wing politicians, who were diligently hiding their true faces. They rightfully say that you can't see the wood for the trees.

I remember, when one night in 2004, I came to the Fantom Café, which was located not far from the Sejm building and I was surprised to see, that everybody was terribly excited. When I asked the bartender, what was happening, he said: *"You know who was here a while ago? A member of Parliament Ziobro!"*

"So what?" I asked. "Anyway, there is no sign, that it's a gay club. He could just make a mistake or to enter by accident," I the understated the matter. Though, when Piotrek, who was then a bartender in the Fantom Café, started to tell me, that the drunken member of the Parliament was trying to pick him up, I got interested. I asked them, if that had any proof. Of course, nobody hit on an idea to take a photo, so the chance to make a noise about that thing went from under our nose. The only effect of that incident was installation of a camera below the bar not to let another occasion go unmissed.

Meanwhile, March came and we had to start organizing the next Equality Parade. But on the horizon, the first dark clouds appeared.

Your own is always better...

The first problems with the Equality Parade began already at the moment of fixing the date. It turned out, that on the 1st of May in Warsaw the European Council was to be held, in connection with which the greater part of the capital city would be blocked. Our march on that day didn't have any chances for a success. I summoned a meeting of the Organizational

Committee to discuss, what to do. I suggested that we should postpone the parade until June. You can imagine my surprise, when I heard Robert Biedroń suggesting, that we should simply cancel the parade. He was trying to convince me, that because the KPH organized the march in Kraków, so the parade in Warsaw was not necessary. That evoked a real indignation in all of us, but Robert Biedroń firmly persisted in his idea. Finally, he withdrew the KPH from the Organizational Committee. For me it was an extremely unpleasant experience, but already then I understood, that the most important thing for Robert Biedroń was the KPH and its promotion.

Finally, we established that the Warsaw parade would be held on 11th June. It was another long weekend after the one in May, what increased the chances for a greater attendance. The preparations were proceeding, while we got from the Kraków chapter of the KPH an official invitation for the March of Tolerance.

In the virtual world, many things were happening, as well. New Web portals and new sites were arising. Jacek Adler couldn't stand idly by, so in March 2004, the Gaylife was established. As for those times, it was a revolutionary idea. The assumption was, that the Gaylife was a dating Portal, but with a wide informational and cultural offer. From the very beginning, Jacek chose to target for the club market. He hit the bull's eye, because up to the moment, most of the existing Web portals didn't devote enough place for the club events and parties. I registered at the Gaylife before the Portal was officially launched. Jacek offered me to help him to test the new product. At first, I was treating that quite distrustfully, but with time I became convinced, that this could be really something good and I engaged into the project with all my heart. In this way, my work for the biggest Polish clubbing Portal began, which lasted nearly for two years.

We went to Kraków in a strong Warsaw team. Jacek Adler with Marcin (both were representatives of the Gaylife's editorial office), Ernest Ivanovs as a representative of the Free Reformed Church and me and Michał Domański, as the representatives of the ILGCN-Poland. At the request of the organizers, we came one day earlier. I remember that we were sitting in a flat of one of the members of the KPH and we were discussing the event that would happen the next day.

The representatives of the organizational committee of the march, were telling us, how they were fighting with the municipality for the last two weeks. It was really bad, for the League of Polish Families and the All-Polish Youth, which were powerful in Kraków, appealed for forbidding the march. When I was listening to the story about the preparations, I started to understand, that our friends from Kraków were at the same point, which we had been in 2001. They were not prepared for the organization of the whole event. While, the questions of securing the conference and the film shows were faultless, the demonstration itself wasn't prepared at all. I was in shock, when I heard the organizers, scorning a potential danger, and claiming that there was no sense to put up groups maintaining order or to organize sound equipment. With my patient persuasion, and a quick telephone to the Kraków division of the APP RACJA, I managed to arrange two portable microphones and stage.

Though, the organizers were still convinced, that nothing was threatening them. The time was to prove, how wrong they were. We agreed that I, as a person who led all the previous parades, would stay close to the leaders, to help them, in case of anything was to happen.

The next morning we went to lay down flowers at the execution wall in Auschwitz. Together with Michał, we were carrying rainbow flags, among which representatives of the non governmental organizations, Ernest in his canonical dress, and the invited guests were walking. After we laid the flowers down, we said a short prayer in memory of the victims and then we quickly visited the museum. I still remember those two hours spent in the barracks of the former concentration camp. The immensity of human atrocity and suffering and of millions of innocent victims engraved in my mind for ever.

On the return back to Kraków we were quiet, sad, and deep in thought. Still, a short conference was awaiting us, and then the first Kraków March of Tolerance.

When we arrived at the rallying-point, I already knew, that there would be much more participants, than the organizers planned. The crowd was growing thicker minute by minute, and the faces of the persons who were appointed to lead the march, reflected a growing panic. At some point, they got completely lost. The police began to urge to set off, because the square, in which we collected couldn't contain all the people willing to take part in the demonstration. I was standing close to Samuel Nowak from the KPH and I was trying to help him to grasp and control the situation. The day was sunny and warm and our portable megaphones weren't able to voice his exclamations properly, Samuel started to loose his voice. Every now and then, he gave me the microphone asking me to shout to instead of him. At some moment, at the back of the column, some commotion arose. There was no way out. I couldn't just stop and wait for the rest of them. So we continued to walk. From time to time, someone from the KPH ran up to me and asked was going on. We were walking through the Kraków's Park. Around us, groups of shaved members of the All-Polish Youth gathered, who had made a good team with the pseudo sport's fans and the nationalists from the National Rebirth of Poland (NOP). When I saw a group from the All-Polish Youth standing under a wall and with their hands raised in a Nazi greeting and shouting: "Gas the gays," immediately, in front of my eyes I saw the gates of the Auschwitz. This is what they want to do with us in Kraków. More or less in the middle of the route, the first eggs were thrown at us, but the police drove away the bandits and we could continue to walk. But it turned out, that we didn't go far.

After having walked another few ten meters, we were stopped by the police cordon, and we were informed, that we had to change our route, because a few hundred meters ahead the counter demonstrators were waiting, and the police wouldn't be able to protect us. The organizes didn't want to consent. They maintained that they had a right to go through the planned route and the police was obliged to protect us. It came to a squabble and only a threat of an immediate dissolving of the demonstration allowed me, together with the orderly officer, to convince the peevish organizers that it was better to change the route and to reach the Wawel taking another way, than to go straight into the arms of the fascist fighting squad of the All-Polish Youth. Thus, we turned into an alley and in a slower pace than so far, we were aiming at the direction of the Wawel's hill. Our goal was the Dragon's Cave, but our opponents were determined not to let us reach it. Among swarms of bald and drunk bandits, wearing bright T-shirts of the All-Polish Youth we continued. The commanders-in-chiefs were the Kraków's aldermen from the League of Polish Families. They were giving commands, which were realized in a disciplined manner. Eggs, bottles and stones were thrown in our direction and some hitting my hair. Katarzyna Kądziela ran up to me and suggested that we should sit down in the middle of the street. On that way, we were to show them, that we were not going to retreat. Unfortunately, it evoked still greater aggression on the part of the opponents. The stones were flying and, what was worse, they started to hit the targets. Fortunately, we moved the banners and streamers to the front of the column, so they served as shields. Most of the projectiles were bouncing from them and they were falling down to the ground not hurting anyone.

At some moment, I felt a powerful blow at my back and I swayed. It turned out, that I was hit with a piece of a brick. Luckily, that was quite a small fragment, which in addition, hit the belt of my rucksack, which I had hung over my shoulder. If not that, the brick would injure my spine. I bended down and I put the piece into my pocket. I keep it to this day as a souvenir.

We were standing opposite each other for a few minutes. The policemen with dogs, shields and the whole antiterrorist equipment were trying to make way for us, but in vain. At one moment, I heard a policeman explaining to a bandit: *"I would let you go, fuck, but, you know, that I'm not allowed."* I saw, that the police weren't on our side. I stated to wonder, how all that might end. After the march, the people had to get home in some way or another. I made contact with the organizers and the officer in charge, and we got to a conclusion, that we would dissolve the demonstration quietly. Thus, the first lines were to stay on the spot, and the people from the back rows would slowly start to disperse home.

Ultimately, on the battlefield only a small group stayed and we slowly started to withdraw in the direction of the City Square. And then, a police cordon broke. A part of the bandits from the fighting squads rushed to combat with the policemen, another part of them rushed to chase us. When I saw a wild ragtag dashing in my direction, waving with chains and baseball bats, I started to look around for a shelter. Unfortunately, every shop and café, which I wanted to enter, slammed the door in my face. Finally, I stack to one of the gates, hoping that I would stay unnoticed. One of the bandits spotted me and began pointing at me with a baseball bat, he yelled: *"That's the fag, who was leading the march. Let's get him, we'll the hit fucker."* A dozen or so musclemen dashed at me. Everything went dark before my eyes and I started to pray silently for help. From the corner of my eye, I managed to notice a police patrol slowly passing by and I felt somebody's hand grasped my arm and at the last moment pulling me into a gate. I heard a bang of the door slamming and the fascists banging on the door. After a while, I understood that Kaśka Kądziela was dragging me up the stairs. It turned out, that we were in an editorial office of the Tygodnik Powszechny, a catholic magazine published in Kraków. Friendly faces were looking at me. Someone asked me, if I was all right and gave me a glass of water. I was all trembling. I had a narrow escape from death and the ones who saved me were journalists representing extremely different social and political views. That was a moment, when I understood, between propagating views and an ordinary human sense of decency. The journalists of the Tygodnik escorted us to the taxi and paid for the way to the hotel.

We were looking for acquaintances and friends through mobiles. We were worried about them. In that way, we learned about a battle which took place on the City Square, during which the fascists, who were fighting with the police, poured over one of the policemen hydrochloric acid. As well, we got to know, that professor Szyszkowska, who took part in the parade, couldn't get safely to the railway station, because the police refused to give her a proper protection. Finally, she was escorted by the municipal police.

Throughout the Polish media, a stormy debate swept the media. The liberal and left wing press condemned the fighting squads. The catholic and right wing press in turn, blame us for the whole event. A pronouncement of one of the cardinals gave me the greatest pain. He stated that the attack on us was justified and praiseworthy. The greatest surprise evoked a reaction of the Kraków's KPH. They accused me of a trial of taking over their march and using it for my own personal goals. Cynicism of those people, who were not capable of assuring the proper security and running the event, I just left that without a comment. I decided, that it was not worth to quarrel with them about that, for those people, who were there seeing, what happened.

No, no, and once more no... JUST LIKE THAT

The time was passing by and I share it among visits in the office of Szyszkowska, working for the party and work in the editorial office of the GayLife. As if by the way of working with professor Szyszkowska, I met Paweł, a lawyer from Jawor, with whom we became very good friends. Thanks to our conversations with him, which sometimes lasted for many hours, I managed to deal with many problems. Also, he taught me many things concerning criminal law and he made me interested in problems fighting juvenile delinquency. I helped him to prepare questionnaires concerning that subject, which he wanted to use in his work in the college.

The turning point for all of us, appeared to be the introduction in the Parliament the bill concerning registration of relationships and passing the bill to be worked out by the Senate commissions. Frequently, I used to resign from other activities and duties and I was going to the Sejm building to fight for subsequent entries of the bill.

It appeared that most of the senators didn't have a slightest idea about the problems of homosexuals. The sittings of the commission were of two kinds, the official ones, at which the following amendments were put to the vote and the working ones, at which they were discussed. At all the working and official sittings Marzena Chińcz from the Web portal Lesbijka.org was with me. Other activists appeared sporadically, most often at the very beginning and the end of the commission's work. That was a tough and difficult combat. We were struggling for nearly every entry, giving up in less significant issues and persisting in the most important ones. The time was passing by and we were slowly coming to an agreement. Basically, we had on our side only professor Szyszkowska and senator Janowska. The rest of the Senate treated our question as a substitute problem and they didn't care about it. Not until the second reading of the bill, uproar was created, mainly due to a presence of Polish media. The Senate Speaker didn't allow me to speak personally, I asked senator Janowska for help. She read off a letter to the parliamentarians on my behalf. We were crossing our fingers till the very end, and when the last, the third, reading of the bill and the voting were held, we knew, that we won the battle. The bill was approved by the Senate and passed on to the Sejm Speaker, who was then Włodzimierz Cimoszewicz from the SLD. And there it tabled even though SLD had campaigned soliciting the gay community for their votes – which they received - and promised to support the bill.

In May, the registration procedure of the Equality Parade 2004 began. I didn't expect major problems, for since the year 2001 we had very good relations with the Town Council, and being the most calm and peaceful demonstration in Warsaw, we collected only praises from the police and the municipal service. Though, this time, the nationalist League of Polish Families, together with its youth association attached to them, which had an inclination towards fascism, both enlivened with their success in Kraków, decided not to allow for the parade in Warsaw. Unfortunately, we found too late, that in the Municipal Council there is someone, who sympathized with the LPR and the APY, who was updating them on our proceedings. That's why, the next day after we had submitted the route of the march, in the Council appeared an application for a counterdemonstration, which was to go the same route and at the same time. Immediately, we suggested a different route, but the APY at once changed theirs also. Those rough tumbles lasted for a few days, until it came to a famous debate in the Życie Warszawy editorial office. They invited Cyprian Gutkowski from the All-Polish Youth, Wojciech Wierzejski, a vice speaker of the Mazovian Sejmik and a member of the LPR, Robert Biedroń, Yga Kostrzewa and me.

The aim of the debate was to determine such two routes of the demonstration, to let them be held legally. While Cyprian Gutkowki was trying to make an impression of an intelligent man, with whom you could reach an agreement, Wojciech Wierzejski shocked even the journalists. He behaved brassily and arrogantly. When the journalists asked him, where our Parade could take place according to him, he answered, that it didn't matter, for wherever it would be held, they were going to get it, that way or another. But he really broke a record of boorishness at the end.

When after the debate had finished, everybody was saying goodbye, he refused to shake hands with Yga, cause as he said, he didn't want to get infected with any disease. Everyone present at the meeting was leaving very embarrassed. While I, just after having got home, submitted an open letter to the leading homophobe of the Polish political scene, in which I informed him, that in response to his boorishness, I was not going to shake his hand any more again. The other people followed my example, and the Wierzejski's e-mail box became flooded with the protest letters. Though he instead of confessing his fault, committed a crime. On his Internet site, he published the list of persons, who had sent a protest to him. He revealed the people's names, second names and e-mails addresses and he named the list: "The list of gays and lesbians, who attack the vice speaker." Immediately, I notified the matter to the Inspector General for the Protection of Personal Data, who secured the site and submitted a notice of an offence at the public persecutor's office. As far, as I know, the matter hasn't been brought to an issue up to this moment, because Wierzejski has been hiding behind various immunities, at first as a Euro-parliamentarian, later as a parliament member of the Sejm of Polish Republic. Though, being in charge of those functions hasn't disturbed him to continue to call upon hatred against homosexual persons.

In 2004, simultaneously, the access referendum, and the elections for the Europarliament, was held, all the events were subordinated to the current political situation. The first one, who took advantage of that was the President of Warsaw, Lech Kaczyński.

Regardless of all our agreements with the Town Council, the police and Municipal Service, he declared, that he wasn't going to give his consent to the Equality Parade, for it posed an act of indecency.

The Media began to be interested in us again. I took part in many press conferences. Even the Catholic Information Agency, and the Radio Józef were trying to reach me to ask me about my opinion. The Polish society divided into two camps, while we initiated the appeal procedures. We were appealing against the Kaczyński's decision for three times. And the Mazovian Voivode for three times annulled the ban. But Kaczyński forbid the Parade for three times, again.

Unfortunately the last time, Kaczyński placed a ban on the parade two days before the planned date of the event and we had no chance for an effective appeal. We received the Voivode's decision post factum. Simultaneously, during that whole war against the President, we were conferring, what to do. There were a few alternative versions of actions. Alter globalists, who discredited Kaczyński in the eyes of the Warsaw citizens before, through having organized a huge demonstration, against which Kaczyński has warned, like against a massacre, while the demonstration appeared to be peaceful, joyful and full of fun, suggested, that we should go illegally. While the KPH demanded from us to call the event off.

Finally, Katarzyna Kądziela from the Office of the Commissioner for Equal Status of Women and Men, convinced me, that an illegal demonstration would only do harm to us. Instead, after having reached agreement with the Workers' Democracy and the Polish Socialist Party, we decided to organize a Freedom Rally. I knew that I couldn't be the person, who submitted the event either as me or as the ILGCN, cause then Kaczyński would forbid it, as well. That's why the demonstration was submitted by the Humanistic Agreement. Though, the whole up-roar had also its merits. Still in May, the publisher of the Gejowo turned to me asking for a meeting and a conversation.

I was distrustful, but we met in one of the Warsaw clubs. Rafał Nawrocki offered me outright to sign an agreement about reconciliation and taking the Parade under his Web portal's patronage. After a moment of hesitation, I agreed and the signed document went into the Internet. One of the effects of the ending of that war was the fact, that all the existing in Poland Internet lesbian and gay Portals were the patrons of the Freedom Rally. But the roughs and tumbles between us and the President of Warsaw, resulted in withdrawing the entire sponsors, except the "Nowy Men" monthly and the "NIE" weekly.

In spite of that, I was preparing for the Rally, strengthened with the support of the Initiative of the Open, a group of open-minded people, who wanted to change something it this world, created by professor Szyszkowska. On the 11th of June, I set off from home in the company of the film production team and Waldek Zboralski and Krzysiek Nowak. Those two wonderful persons were to support me many times in my activities. Besides, Waldek was one of the first Polish gays, who were acting in the organizations. Together with the others, he founded The Warsaw Homosexual Movement, the first, then still illegal LGBT organization in Poland. He was oppressed in the Action Hyacinth and to this day he felt a strong trauma concerning the ways of exercising power by the authorities. We are very good friends. On the 11th of June, he and Krzysiek were acting as my bodyguards. Because earlier, I got a few letters with threats and someone was shooting at me twice near my home.

We met with the rest of the organizers at the Bankowy Square. Just then, I met Waldemar Kocoń, a wonderful singer, in love with wild cats, who came back to Poland after many years of travels abroad. Being a keen democrat, he decided to give us support in our struggle and he lent us the sound system and the stage, which was placed opposite the city hall. Around 13:00, the people started to gather. There were not as many of them, as the last year, because the policy of frightening led by the All-Polish Youth and the Law and Justice (PiS) brought negative results. Nevertheless, around 1 000 people gathered at the square. Our opponents were hardly seen. The only visible element was a van with antiunion slogans standing nearby. We began with playing through the loudspeakers an official hymn of the Equality Parade, which was composed especially for the occasion last year. Later, the speeches followed. In the meantime, I was taken aside by a production team of the First Program of the Polish Television, to record a short interview. When I was answering the questions, suddenly, a man came, and stood behind me and pored a bowl of whipped cream mixed with wallpaper glue. He did it before the eyes of the policemen and the Polish Television cameras. Of course, the police didn't react, when he was slowly leaving the square. Kasia

Kądziela dashed to help me. She helped me to wipe up from the mixture and started to look for a T-shirt for me for a change. I had on me a black T-shirt with a pink triangle on the back and my national identification. At some moment, my black jacket was all in eggs and the yolk was flowing down in the front. When I reached the stage, Katarzyna Matuszewska from the Labor Union, who was coordinating the order of the speakers, gave me a microphone, and I told the people, what had just happened. I showed them my dirty T-shirt and I said that if the League of Polish Families wanted to put us to jail and cure us using gas, I didn't want to make troubles and I already made a prison uniform for myself. After the speech, I changed my T-shirt. I got dressed in one with a lesbian symbol, which I got from Marzena Chińcz and I listened to the others' speeches. The words, that I remember the most, were coming from Ernest's speech. He said pointing to the sky: "*Look, yesterday, during the procession for the Corpus Christi in Warsaw it was raining heavily. Today, it is beautiful sunshine. God is with us, because God is Love. And we fight for the right to Love.*" He received hot applause from the crowd. After the demonstration, I went to the Police Headquarters to submit a notice about commission of a crime by a man, who poured a mixture with cream and glue on me at the Rally. I told them, that his face was registered by cameras, so there will be no problem to find him. Unfortunately, the police didn't want to see to the matter and after some time, they discontinued the case due to lack of detection of the perpetrator. Anyway, all the cases I submitted at the police through all those years finished in the same way. They have never caught either the one, who mugged me, shoot at me or insulted me. The police was not interested in helping a gay. Not much has changed in this matter to this day.

Until the end of the year 2004, we were trying together with the APP RACJA to collect signatures under a motion for a referendum concerning recalling of Kaczyński from the function of the President of Warsaw, but we didn't manage to collect enough votes. The bill concerning registration of partner relationships got stuck in the desk of Cimoszewicz and in spite of many trials, we didn't manage to take it from there. The SLD lost its interest in helping the LGBT community, the more, that the priority far them became elections for the Euro-parliament and the next year, the presidential elections of the Polish Republic.

The result was such, that according to the opinion pools, their support was successively falling, and we were loosing hope. The only change, that we managed to fight out in the Polish law, was a bequest in the labor law forbidding discrimination with regard to sexual orientation. After the partition and founding a club of the Social Democratic Party of Poland (SDPL), SLD wasn't interested in implementation of the equality politics.

In November, the first equality march was held in Poznań. I was invited to take part in the conference as a panelist. I came especially one day earlier and, as it was in Kraków, I met organizers with a total lack of preparation for the march, that was going to be held the next day. There was no group of people responsible for keeping order, and there was only one microphone, and the organizers asked me to help them in case they needed me. I knew what this would lead to.

The march in Poznań hasn't gone even a few meters. Admittedly, the police sheltered us effectively from the fascists from the All-Polish Youth, but finally they made us turn back and hold a stationary demonstration on the stairs of the Castle. Later, again, I was accused of a will to boss. Maybe, indeed, it wasn't worth to interfere, but on the other hand, I don't know, if I would be able to forgive myself, if I hadn't reacted and had let it to come to a tragedy. Anyway, I was never again invited for any march organized later by the KPH or the Greens. Those people decided that they knew better, how to organize marches. As the events of the following years showed, the bravado didn't pay.

For the bigger part of the year, a plebiscite organized by the Web portal Lesbijka.org of choosing a homosexual and heterosexual Person of the Rainbow, the two people the most meritorious for the LGBT movement. Every organization, every Web portal and newspaper taking part in the action, could nominate their candidates. While, everyone, who had access to the Internet or to the newspapers, could take part in the voting, when the results were made public, I understood that my world started to shrink slowly. I also understood the advantage of having money and a deceptive persona meant. The heterosexual Person of the Rainbow became, what was obvious for everyone, Professor Maria Szyszkowska. I lost against Robert Biedroń with a fraction of a percent for the homosexual of the year award. Before that, the association form Kraków awarded him for building tolerance in Poland. Then, for another time, I saw for myself, that there was nothing more transient, than human memory.

During all those political and social perturbations, I was observing attentively the actions of Jacek Adler and the Gaylife. As some point, I started to send him texts for publication and soon we came to a conclusion, that I should become an editor of the Gaylife. We signed an appropriate agreement and I started working for the Web portal as an official editor. I also bought a digital camera, to be able to make current coverage from the events in clubs. Though, I derived income from other sources. In Warsaw a new club was founded, the Synkret, and I engaged there as an organizer of the events. All the year 2004, I was running a cyclic night of stars. As well, I managed to invite a heavy metal band and Waldemar Kocoń to the Synkret. Together with Jacek Adler, we organized another Christmas Eve for the Solitary Lesbians and Gays in the Synkret.

That was a beautiful ceremony, at which, unfortunately, Ernest was missing - he had to leave the country. Some of those people came to us only because they were looking for power and praise. Also, there happened to be persons mentally unbalanced. As a consequence of slanders, intrigues and arguments, our first community came apart. In consequence, all of us suffered.

I was intrigued with a young Pentecostal pastor. I also was trying to take up studies at the Christian Theological Academy in Warsaw, but unfortunately, my funds were sufficient only for the first semester. I had to cope with everything by myself. Thus, the year 2005 came; the most critical year for me, as far as my life and activity was concerned.

Though, before we could celebrate another clamorous New Year's Eve, on the 5th of December an agreement of the Union of the Left (UL) had been signed. This was an informal coalition of many leftist communities, which wanted to be an alternative for the government of the SLD and the SDPL. I remember, that at the ceremony of signing the agreement, an older man came up to me and asked, if he could talk to me. Of course, I said yes. We went to a corner of the hall, where another older man was waiting. He introduced me as his life partner. They shared the facts that they, both professors, were a couple for over forty years. I envied them very sincerely. I knew how difficult their life must have been in the times of profound communism, persecutions and repressions.

**You must respect me.
Your hate for me is only thing
what keeps you together**

Time of questions and the answers...

On the second of January 2005, I cut my hair. Ultimately, Janusz Sztyber convinced me to do so. I remember when I left the barber with feeling naked, I was aiming at a bus stop, and on the way, I was saying to myself, that now it would be better, for I would be less recognizable in the street, thus also I will be safer. My hopes were soon shattered by an old woman, who approached me at the bus stop and said: *"Mr. Szymon, wouldn't you be so nice and give me a few zlotys for dinner?"*

In my life then, many changes were happening. First of all, the Union of the Left of the Third Polish Republic was being founded. It was an initiative of a few persons from small parties, who came to a conclusion, that it would be better to unite their forces than to let the louder and louder right wing, ultimately finish the Polish left wing. In that initiative, a chairperson of the Labor Union, and the Minister of Work and Social Policy Izabella Jaruga Nowacka was in the lead. Thus, I devoted my time to working on organization of events in the Synkret club and to writing the party's platform. At some point, I started to share the first of those activities with Marcin Mich. Our cooperation was shaping up so well, and his constant travels from the place near Warsaw, where hew lived, were becoming a bigger and bigger nuisance, that finally I decided, that the best solution would be to rent him a room in my flat in return for a part of the and rent and hired him for keeping the place in order. In this way, Marcin and Jacek became an inseparable part of my life for the next year and a half.

Meanwhile, the ILGCN-Poland was slowly collapsing. Everybody expected from me, that I would tend to everything. The people were not used to acting independently, and when I ran out of motivation, they simply started to leave. That's why I was listening with interest to an offer that

One day, Tomasz Bączkowski then unknown to Polish gay community, he permanently lived in Germany and was a friend of Robert Biedron the president of KHP (Campaign Against Homophobia.) Tomasz alleged that he worked with some German associations, which were organizing Europride at the time. He said, that the key issue with the organization of parades was money. That's why he unfolded a vision of thousands of Euro, which the foreign sponsors were ready to donate. Though, he said, that the only conditions of the donations would be creating one organization, which would take care exclusively of organizing parades. He maintained that bringing to life another association was no sense, and he suggested creating a foundation. He explained that at the moment, when the three biggest organizations LGBT create a foundation, then gaining the funds and the organizing of the Equality Days would be simple. I had doubts, for the ILCGN didn't have any funds that they would be able to assign as an initial fund. But Bączkowski was trying to convince me, that it wasn't a problem, for he himself was ready to give to the ILGCN the necessary sum of money, in case it was needed. He also declared that he would cover all the costs of bringing the foundation into existence, under a condition, that he would become its chairman.

Because the name of the Parade and the Equality Days was registered in the charter of the ILGCN and thus, it was a subject to the law protection, so we needed a positive decision of the management of the Association. Thus, I summoned a meeting and we agreed the conditions. The basic condition was the presence of two members of the ILGCN in the Foundation Council. The charter of the Foundation was created in cooperation of KPH and Lambda Warsaw. In February 2005, we met in the notary public's office and we brought the foundation into being. If I had known, what effects that could have, I would have let them cut off my right hand not to sign any more documents. But then I was so preoccupied with all that was happening in my life, that I let myself trust Tomasz Bączkowski and Robert Biedron. The foundation began to take shape and I spent my time on other duties.

In the course of works over the platform of the Union of the Left, disagreements appeared. The project promoted by Jaruga Nowacka was very from the part connected with people's outlook on life and it resembled a program of the Labor Union mixed together with the program of the SLD. Many people didn't like it, and in spite of the explanations, that it was only a provisional platform, prepared for the needs of the Founding Congress, it evoked disputes. Growing tension made subsequent parties was leaving the Union of the Left. For me personally, the greatest disappointment was the resignation of Professor Maria Szyszkowska from the honor patronage. I have to admit with sadness, that the way she has been treated during the consultations, didn't leave her any other choice. Though, I did believe, that after the congress, the program could be improved.

As well, I strongly defended bi-partisanship, which enabled many persons to be a member of the UL without having to resign from their home parties. Though, I was sure, that division of the left wing in the situation, when consecutive scandals caused a long-lasting fall of the Left in the polls, would be a major mistake. In that question, I supported Piotr Musiał, the chairman of the APP RACJA, who saw the chance of the Reason in the unification.

At the founding congress, I was elected practically unanimously the vice chairperson of the Union of the Left of the Third Republic of Poland. The media observed with great surprise, that here, for the first time in Poland, an openly homosexual person took such a high political position. I also became a member of the Policy Council, which was to draft the program by the time of the Election Convention at the end of the year.

That year also included the death of John Paul II. The country of Poland got overcome with grief. I even managed to convince the members of the National Council of the APP RACJA to send condolences in connection with that fact. That was my last activity in that party. In connection with the mourning, the Campaign Against Homophobia called off the march in Kraków. And then, yet again, Łukasz Pałucki surfaced. Backing himself up with the LGBT Foundation, which actually existed only on paper, he announced that the march was going to be held. A wave of criticism rolled through the media. Pałucki not only didn't want to respect the people's grief, but also he clearly decided to make a name for himself thanks to a tasteless provocation. What's worse, the provocation was so ineffectually prepared, that the Municipal Council had no trouble in finding an excuse to forbid the demonstration because of formal reasons.

The journalists, who were questioning me, if I was going to appear in Kraków, weren't surprised, when I informed them, that I didn't support that kind of controversial exploiting of human feelings. Robert Biedroń showed even bigger anger, when he shouted out to the whole world, that Pałucki had stolen the march from him. I should have marked that outburst then, but it escaped my attention in the course of events.

In Kraków, a very powerful group fighting against homosexuals came into play. For the first time, the priest Piotr Skarga Association surfaced in the media in 2004, at the occasion of sending leaflets opposing the legalization of the partner relationship. The source of finances of that organization has remained a secret, but in 2005 they flooded Poland with leaflets delivered to homes by post. They boasted that they sent a few thousand of them. Those leaflets were steeped in hatred. In some, there were disgusting comparisons of homosexuality to zoophiles,__necrophilia and other sexual deviations.

Meanwhile, Tomasz Bączkowski at consecutive meetings of the Equality Foundation Council proposed enterprising plans of inviting the big music stars for the Equality Parade. He was tantalizing us by promises of great contacts and money. Meanwhile, a conference organized by the Campaign Against Homophobia was coming to the foreground. That conference was to precede the parade and become the germ of international debate on the rights of gays and lesbians in Poland. At some point, I noticed that Tomasz Bączkowski stopped talking about the music stars and the subject of the parade was dying down somehow. The matter came up again just before the official deadline of submitting of the demonstration to the city authorities.

The President of Warsaw, Lech Kaczyński, who had publicly declared his readiness to stand for the presidential election that year, reacted hysterically to every mention about the approaching parade. He said he would forbid the parade still before the official motion came in to the city council. The Foundation's authorities didn't know what to do. A rerun from 2004 was in prospect. At one of the meetings of the Council, I suggested to submit a dozen or so stationary demonstrations, among which people could walk one by one, in this way creating an informal parade. At first, my idea was criticized by Bączkowski and Biedroń, but with time it gained approval, and after another ban of Kaczyński, it was put into practice. Unfortunately, neither they, nor me could expect, that Kaczyński would go the extreme. Having broken the Constitution and all the legal principles, he forbade most of the rallies submitted by private persons. Proposals submitted by All-Polish Youth and one of ours were accepted and that our gathering was to be held near the Sejm building. The decision concerning the ban was delivered to us by the municipal authorities at a conference on the day before the Parade. And then, against Katarzyna Kądziela's opinion, we started to put pressure on Bączkowski, to go in the parade, despite everything. Meanwhile, the conference was in progress. I was taking part in it as a panelist of the discussion over the homosexual culture.

The whole conference, in spite of the presence of many foreign guests, was dominated with the panelists from the KPH. During the conference, Robert Biedroń approached me and gave me an invitation for one person for a banquet after the conference. I asked him, if he couldn't give one more, for Janusz, who was a vice chairman of the ILGCN. He said, that no, for it was a banquet exclusively for foreign guests and only organizers were to take part in it.

When I came to the banquet, much to my surprise, I found there the full management of the Campaign and the Lambda Warsaw, plus a considerable number of the people, whom I didn't know and who said they were members of the KPH or volunteers from the Foundation. There were plenty of food, alcohol and other goodies. There were even representatives of the media, who were recording interviews with Robert and Tomasz. Also, many foreign guests showed up. Katarzyna Kądziela told me, that Ryszard Kalisz, the Minister of the Interior, gave the Police order to guarantee the demonstrators safety, irrespective of what was going on. For me, that was a sign that we could walk safely. I couldn't stay long at the banquet, for the next day the parade was going to be held. I went home.

In the morning, I came under the Sejm, where a few thousand people gathered. I started to look out for Bączkowski and Biedroń. I found them near the microbus with a few small loud speakers. When I asked them, why they didn't have a normal equipment, they answered that they got it from a German foundation and that it would be just enough. Of course, I don't have to add, that through those microscopic loud speakers, you could hear nothing except a wild noise made by a huge crowd of people, and a big group of the All-Polish Youth, who were chanting their slogans under a monument opposite the Sejm. After the incomprehensive for any one speeches delivered by Bączkowski, Biedroń, Jaruga Nowacka and a few other guests, we set off.

At first, we were to walk down the pavement, but the police asked us to move to the street because they were not able to control the people. So, to the Plac Trzech Krzyży, we were walking along one lane of the street.

After we entered the Nowy Świat Street, the police closed for us the entire street, explaining, that it was the best solution. Thus, we were walking further, in the direction of the Świętokrzyska Street, when the fascist hit squads approached. But when they saw, that we exceeded their numbers, they started to grasp at straws to stop us. They were sitting in the street, they created living chains, and they were throwing at us bottles and eggs. The police intervened by moving them from the street and isolating them from us. When we were reaching the Palace of Culture and Science, ahead of the front of the Equality Parade, a cordon of the All-Polish Youth was walking. Later it was pushed back by the police behind the Palace.

Under the Palace, on the improvised platform, where Le Madame Club provided a professional PA system, subsequent speeches were delivered. When they let me say something as one of the last speakers, I thanked everybody for fulfilling my dream about the people coming out into the street to fight for their rights. I also commented on the presence of the opponents, saying that today my another great dream was fulfilled, for the first time the All-Polish Youth was walking at the head of the Equality Parade. The participant's of the Parade burst out laughing, while the opponents started to shout. When it all ended, we came back to our homes.

The year 2005 was very special for Poland. There were a parliamentary and a presidential elections waiting for us. Everything was going on very quickly and with abandon. When within the Union of the Left, a powerful front arose, which was striving for forming an election coalition with the SLD, we knew, that the only solution for some members of the RACJA would be to leave the parent party and becoming a member of the Union of the Left. Meanwhile, the UL was holding coalitional talks with the SLD.

The price that we had to pay for that alliance was supporting Włodzimierz Cimoszewicz in the presidential election, the same parliament member, who before effectively blocked in the Sejm the bill concerning registration of the partner relationships. At first, we wanted to support Maria Szyszkowska, who believed she had a chance for presidency. We gave her our support as the ILGCN and we were trying to help with collecting signatures. Though, I knew, she had no chance to win.

When it turned out, that she hadn't managed to collect the required number of signatures, she hailed me and Robert Biedron as traitors. It hurt me very much, in contrast to the others, I've never treated her as an object and I've always tried to help her with everything. Unfortunately, the team of the people she chose, connected with the RACJA, who were to promote her, appeared to be not only totally ineffective, but just the opposite, they hurt her career so, as she missed the chance to return in politics. Her run in the election to the Sejm also was a washout. So was our coalition with the SLD.

Soon, it turned out, that we didn't have any chance for good places on the ballots. Bartłomiej Morzycki, who was doing his duty as a chairman of the party, didn't manage negotiations effectively, while Izabela Jaruga Nowacka was interested exclusively in her first place on the election list. At first, I was proposed a place in Warsaw, but knowing, that Robert Biedroń would run for the Sejm, I refused and at the same time I agreed to the last place on the ballot in Wrocław.

Unfortunately, my health started to get worse. The constant stress, sitting up till late at night, and oceans of coffee, made my ulcer arrack later, another serious disease happened. Though, before my health totally broke down, a scandal, in which Robert Biedroń and the Gaylife Portal played a part, erupted. Eventually, that thing ruined me physically and mentally.

Jacek Adler of GayLife has never liked Robert Biedroń. He expressed his dislike through malicious articles many times. Though, in 2005 he got an irrefutable argument straight into his hand. The thing was about the Equality Parade, which ended a short time ago and the way it was funded. The Equality Foundation designated the funds gathered for the Parade, practically for the conference and banquet. Thousands of Euros was spent, whereas at the

Parade itself, which was to be the most important element of the feast, there wasn't even a proper sound system. Besides, the Foundation was trying to conceal that fact scrupulously, through not publishing the official settlement from their activities. Robert Biedroń didn't focus on clearing the whole thing up, but on attacking me instead. He admitted that in the Polish politics, there was no place for two strong gay personalities. So he decided to destroy me. He threatened me, that if I didn't force Jacek to remove the article from the Gaylife, he would convince the SLD to cross me out from the list of the candidates on the ballot. In addition, Katarzyna Kądziela engaged into the whole thing. She was trying to convince me to carry out his demands. But before Robert managed to fulfill his threats my health got worse, one night I was taken to the Czerniakowski hospital. There, the doctor diagnosed me with acute hepatitis and he sent me to an isolation hospital. I only managed to call my mum, Piotr Musiał and Marzena Chińcz from the Web portal Lesbijka.org.

It was Piotr, who informed the SLD about my decision about resignation from running for parliament, and Marzena transmitted the message to the community. I was lying in the hospital room and was praying for a miracle. And a miracle happened; instead of hepatitis C, the doctors diagnosed me with the B type. One o the first telephone calls I got in the hospital was from Robert Biedroń, who asked me how I was. I told him, that I had viral hepatitis B which was what the doctors told me. He quickly said good bye. A few days later, a trusted friend informed me, that someone in Warsaw was spreading rumors that I was dying of AIDS. The only person from the community, who knew, in which hospital I was, was Robert Biedroń. So, I didn't have to look for the source of that gossip.

For that month, which I spent in hospital, only my mum, Bartek, a friend from the Union of the Left, Karolina, a friend from college, and a boy, whom I met through the Gaylife, visited me. The rest of my friends and acquaintances weren't interested in my fate. That gave me much food for thought. I was spending my time on reading the books that my mum was delivering to me, on going for walks and writing on the laptop. Basically, I felt as I were in a sanatorium, the treatment was limited to receiving vitamin B and blood control. My organism was to fight the virus by itself. I managed to achieve that after one year of being on a diet and taking vitamins.

After I had left the hospital, I was observing the pre-election fight and I knew, that my worst fears were fulfilling. A coalition PiS-PO, on which everybody was counting, though I firmly repeated, that Jarosław Kaczyński would strive for the coalition with the Self-Defense and the League of Polish Families.

Nobody believed me, but unfortunately, the time proved, I was right. The political fight started to use dangerous methods, which so far had never been utilized in Poland. One of them was to strike strongly the homosexual community.

Law and Justice decided to make use of a dislike towards homosexuals and to make a public enemy out of them. The first attack was, of course, opposition to the Equality Parade, and after that another oppositions came. The march in Poznań in November 2005 was brutally dispersed by the police, who instead of arresting our opponents chanting fascist slogans, was beating with truncheons the demonstrators demanding freedom and tolerance. That happened already after the parliamentary and presidential elections were won by the PiS. Though, before that came to the march and the police's action, something else happened.

A few days before the second round of the presidential elections, in Warsaw, an antiterrorist alarm was announced. It turned out, that a few editorial offices received an anonymous letter signed by a Super Queer and Power Gay. Immediately, Lech Kaczyński used that in his election campaign, which brought him a victory.

Please, confess something!
Minister of Justice has press conference next hour!

I was bombard with telephone calls asking me, if I had to do anything with that thing. I was shocked, the more, that two policemen entered my flat and asked me about my life, my connections with terrorism and about other gay activists. They also informed me in passing, that most probably the police would begin a repetition of the operation Hyacinth. This was an operation in 1985 where they detained a few thousand homosexuals, interrogated them and established their dossier, later called the pink archives. In spite of having a picture of the person, who sent that e-mail, and having determined a reward for catching him, the police haven't managed to pick up the trail of the offenders. Instead, I was summoned to appear at the police and in the public persecutor's office in order to submit clarification. Every time, I repeated exactly the same things. A month of piece used to follow, and I was summoned again. After the election had been won by the PiS, (Law and Justice) nobody asked a question, who benefited from that whole action -- it was Lech Kaczyński.

Being disheartened with the continuous attacks on me I proffered resignation from the function of the chairman of the Association. At the same time, I stressed, that I was at the association's disposal and as an Ambassador of the Polish Culture attached to the ILGCN Poland; I would continue to be involved in the activities in defense of the homosexual persons' rights.

After the National Convention of the Union of the Left, Izabella Jaruga Nowacka together with her supporters left us, I became the Vice Chairman of the party. The year 2005 was slowly coming to an end. The PiS took over the power in Poland, destroying, among other things, the anchor of an artistic gay spirit of the capital city, which was the nightclub Le Madame, creating subsequent scandals. Meanwhile, in November, I joined the Web portal JoeMonster.org, on which I could rest from the nutty reality in the haze of joyful absurd. Simultaneously, I continued my cooperation with the Gaylife, I visited clubs and I was trying to sort out my life anew. As well, I took up the artistic acts of photography. At first, I was doing that to meet the needs of my own gallery, later for Jacek Adler. I surrounded myself with the acquaintances and friend whom I met through his Web portal and I hoped that I was free from problems, at least for some time. Soon, I got to know, how wrong I was.

Something comes to an end, and something is beginning...

On the first of January 2006 at my home, a ceremonial church service of the Free Reformed Church was held, during which I was ordained a deacon. It was a great experience for me. A few days later, journalists called me asking, if I was aware, that my personal data had been published on a fascist site of the Blood and Honor association, together with threats against me. When I checked that information, it turned out, that I landed on the "honorable" first place in the list of the Warsaw "queer enemies of the white race." I informed the Inspector General for the Protection of Personal Data (GIODO), the Police and the

Public Persecutor's office. In spite of a big interest of media, the security services were not quite interested in chasing the perpetrators until the moment, when in Warsaw an attempt of murder of a person from the list took place. In the course of the inquiry lasting one year, the Polish Police hadn't been able to block the Internet site, not to mention apprehending the offenders. The whole procedure was limited to summoning us for interrogations and to attempts made to convince us to withdraw the charges. Again, the same questions concerning my life, my acquaintances and other gay activists appeared. Admittedly, a few persons suspected of creating the site were detained, but as time proved, that was no use. The site appeared again on the Web and it was continuously updated. In spite of threats against me, and even an attempt of arson of my flat, I was trying to lead a normal life.

One day, I got an e-mail from my father, in which he informed me, that he was expecting his daughter to be born. I was shocked, but at the same time, I was very happy, that he decided to get in touch with me. After such a long period of silence between us, the time came to build the family bonds. After the childbirth, I visited the hospital and in this way I met Asmee and Salma - my father's partner and their lovely daughter. We started to talk and I noticed how much my father changed from the time of our angry parting. I don't know, it was the influence of time, or Asmee, but we had a good contact again. When a few months later he went down very seriously with cancer, I was praying heartily for his recovery. And he did it. True, he will never be fully healthy, but he survived, and after all, that's the most important thing.

After they closed down the Synkret, I joined up with the Galeria club and continued working for the Gaylife as a photojournalist and a photographer. I was doing at least one session a month. I signed a contract with every model, containing a clause concerning a potential resignation of the model from the cooperation. As a result, that clause led to breaking the cooperation with Jacek Adler and my decision concerning establishing my own Web portal.

Jacek didn't pay me for the photographs and articles. The contract between us guaranteed to me, that in exchange for working for free, I would have an access to the Portal's administration and a possibility of publishing my texts signed with my own name. It wasn't much, but for me it was a possibility of sharing my emotions and thoughts with a wider audience. At the same time, I was publishing the sessions of the male acts on my Internet site, which attracted quite a few users, but it didn't bring in any profits. At one point, one of the models, whose photos I published, acting under pressure from his family, asked me to remove his pictures. In accordance to the contract we had signed, he was to pay me compensation. We fixed the amount of money and I informed Jacek about the necessity of removing the pictures of that model from the Gaylife's gallery. Jacek said that he wanted half of the money for himself. I agreed and I went to the Gallery to sign an annex to the contract. Much to my surprise, after I came home and entered the Gaylife, I found out that I was deprived of my network administration powers. I, being furious, called Jacek, I heard, that he did it preventively, cause he was afraid, that I would remove the pictures and wouldn't give him the money.

That was the last drop of bitterness, which filled the cup to the brim. Because in this way, Jacek broke off an agreement between us and he hurt me with his suspicions, I informed him, that I no longer was going to work for him for free. I took the money from the model, I gave half of that to Jacek, and I demanded that he removed all the pictures made by me from the Portal, as well, as he removed my name from the publisher's imprint. I deleted my account myself. At the same time, after talking to my friends, I decided, that the time came to establish my own Web portal. The Gaylife was inexorably heading towards a pornographic Portal, because Jacek, the author of most of the texts, wrote mainly about sex clubs and sex events. I didn't want my name be connected with such texts, all the more so because according to me, sex events had not much to do with club parties. In February 2006 I registered a company LGBT Press and I started to look for someone, who would create a Portal I had in mind. Out of a few offers, I chose the one recommended by one of my colleagues from college. As it turned out later, the company made me a Portal, which didn't meet my expectations and cost a large amount of money. Unfortunately, I signed a contract and I committed myself to pay. For a few following months, I was paying installments for the product, which a few months later I deleted myself from the server. From that moment, the Acoto.pl, that's how I called my Web portal, has been undergoing alterations, cause thanks to my acquaintances I found another computer specialist.

You've served you purpose, we don't need you any more...

From the beginning of the year, every time I met Robert Biedroń in the clubs, I was trying to get to know, what was going on with the Equality Parade and why the meetings of the Foundation Council didn't take place. Every time, Robert informed me, that he wasn't in touch with Bączkowski and he himself didn't know, what was going on. I didn't get any answer for my many e-mails sent to the Foundation asking about the progress in the preparations. One day I noticed, that the worker of the Foundation responsible for a musical setting was Łukasz Pałucki. I expected problems, but nobody paid attention to my warning.

When on the 1st of April, Web portal Homiki.pl placed a humorous text untitled "ABC of a homo," under the letter A was an entry "Ambassador" with a description of me. The text itself, as for the April Fools' Day, was funny and interesting. It was the commentaries underneath which appeared to me much more interesting. Łukasz Pałucki, for example, stated, that a procedure of recalling me from the function of the Ambassador of Polish Culture attached to the ILGCN. I laughed at the information. I knew that Bill Schiller had appointed Marcin Śmietana and Olga Chajdas as the ambassadors and he had never mentioned recalling anybody. In an unrefined way, Łukasz imputed ignorance of English to me and stated, that he knew better what was going on in the West. As it turned out two weeks later, indeed, he knew better.

When in Moscow, the authorities forbade the march of homosexuals, and the march was held illegally, of course, Tomasz Bączkowski and Łukasz Pałucki were present there. One day after all the Portals had published the coverage of those events, a notice made by Łukasz Pałucki that he replaced me on the position of the Ambassador. He didn't mention a word about any other ambassador and he focused on criticizing me. When I protested, he answered, that he was surprised with that nomination, as well. Wonders never cease! After I had consulted Bill Schiller, I learned, that Łukasz Pałucki together with Bączkowski informed him in Moscow, that I stopped acting at all, that I was seriously ill and I should be removed urgently. Unfortunately, Bill believed them. At the same time, I noticed, that the logo of the ILGCN vanished from the Parade's site. Bączkowski explained that we didn't pay for being on the list. The statute of the Foundation or his previous declarations didn't matter for him. My name vanished from the history of the Parades described on their site, whereas Bączkowski started to introduce himself as a creator of the Equality Parade in Poland. In all the pictures, next to him was always Robert Biedroń and Łukasz Pałucki. One month before the Parade, I officially asked for placing my web Portal to the list of the media patrons. In return, I was asked for a meeting with Bączkowski, who informed me, that my Web portal might become a patron under a condition, that I would pay them minimum 300 zlotys. On the same day, I met the publisher of the AYOR monthly, who informed me, that they didn't request one single zloty from him. I got the same information from several Web portals and private sites from the list of the patrons. When I asked Robert Biedroń about the whole situation, he said, that he didn't know anything. He described the whole thing in the Gaylife. Bączkowski's reaction to the text was accusing me of an attempt of wangling tickets for a concert after the Parade out of him. I knew that the most important thing was an idea of the Parade, so I decided not to take the case to court. In the meantime, many interesting things were happening.

Having more free time, I was staying long on various gay Web portals. At one of them, I met an American artist named Lee Andrew. We were talking much on photography and models. At some point, I invited him to Poland. He agreed and after some time, he showed up in Warsaw from his home in Italy. There is an anecdote connected with his coming. His arrival coincided with the pope's Benedict XVI, who came to Poland with his first pilgrimage, leaving Warsaw. The polish security service was unprecedented not known before in our country. The airport, from which the pope was to leave, was closed 4 hours before and 2 after his departure. We spent together a total of 6 hours waiting for the moment they would let us leave the airport. When we got home, my American friend couldn't understand why so strange regulations were in force in my country. To tell you the truth, he still cannot understand Polish mentalities.

During my spring stay in Berlin, where I was taking part in an anti-global conference devoted to the rights of homosexual persons in Poland, I met a young lesbian, who asked me for help in organizing young German lesbians and gays to Warsaw for the Parade. I promised to help her and we established a contact, which effect was an arrival of 250 young Germans.

We placed them in the Galleria nightclub, which accommodated that crowd without difficulty. My friends from the Acoto and the Gaylife took care of food, and I was busy with service and interpreting. Lee Andrew and Janusz Sztyber were helping me with that. Everone was waiting for the Parade, which was to begin. An ecumenical church service which I was to celebrate before the Parade, couldn't take place, because there was simply not enough place in the Gallery.

And time, as well. That's why I restricted myself to a short blessing and together with my two hundred and fifty charges we went in the direction of the Sejm building. On our way we met another group from Germany, which joined us. I was leading nearly two thousand people, other people from Warsaw, hurrying for the Parade, joined us, as well. When, in spite of minor problems, we got to the Sejm building, the Parade was just beginning. Together with my friends, I was walking under a banner of the Free Reformed Church, in which a quote from the Gospel was saying: "Have no fear." I approached the platform of the organizers thinking, that when Robert Biedroń spots me, he would let me to deliver a speech, what we used to do every year. Indeed, he spotted me, but instead of calling me, he turned to the crowd and parodying a trembling voice of John Paul II, he quoted the slogan from our banner. Then I understood that according to them, there was already no place for me in the Parade. I retreated to the back of the column and together with another Christian group I was walking at the end. My friends were transported with joy on our way; they were taking photos and filming our march. Several times along the way, we met groups of fascists from the All-Polish Youth and other right wing organizations, who were throwing eggs and bottles with water at us and were shouting out some racist and homophobic slogans. At some moment, it came to a scuffle, during which, as it turned out, two people from the German group, which I had in my care were involved.

I was informed about what happened only when the Parade ended and I immediately notified Tomasz Baczkowski about that. I counted, that he, as an organizer, should investigate. Unfortunately, I heard that it wasn't his problem and I shouldn't bother him about it. My German friends had to manage with the problem themselves.

We helped them to contact the Embassy and send them home. We went back home very tired ourselves. I felt sorry, for I comprehended fully, that Tomasz Baczkowski together with Robert Biedroń and Łukasz Pałucki slowly and successively were erasing my name from the history of the LGBT movement in Poland. Though, I didn't have as much power as before to defy that. All the time, I wasn't in the best of health after the disease. Additionally, discouraged by the constant attacks against me, I needed to have a rest. When I heard, that Bączkowski was given an award for building tolerance in Poland, and for creating the Equality Parade, I came to conclusion, that it was time to move aside. At the same time, I wasn't surprised, when I read the information, that all the money which he collected fir the Parade, ended up on his private bank account. Then, I understood, that people were capable of doing anything to gain money and a moment of fame. I decided not to have anything to do with that, never again.

When they stop talking about you...

Working together with Lee Andrew, I learnt to look at my life from a different prospective. I understood, that if I don't look after myself, nobody would care, what was happening to me. Gradually, I was moving aside from the community. I stopped visiting the clubs, which took effect - a gossip about my fatal disease spread. One of my former partners even started to spread rumors, that he saw a medicine against AIDS at my flat and that I was dying. At one time, I would argue and try to straighten and clear up the gossips. But now, I simply cooped myself up and worked. In the second half of the year, my first amateur DVD with my sessions recorded was published. I started up a gallery and my own blog. I laughed my head off, when I saw, that two months later Robert Biedroń started his blog. Apparently, he didn't want to be worse than me even in that matter.

Still before the Parade, I confined to Lee Andrew my great dream that was opening a center of queer center in Warsaw. I wanted the capital of our country had a place, where every lesbian or gay, a bisexual or transsexual with no obstacles could find information for themselves, help and support. I knew that the office of the Lambda was constantly threatened with the right wing municipal authorities and only an office completely independent had a chance to sustain. Lee Andrew drew my attention to the fact, that most of similar centers in the West were connected with an activity of the clubs, and the clubs reaped their profit from it. We came to a conclusion, that we need such a place. This was how the Queer Central Station. We decided to fulfill our dream.

But to do that, we have to raise the proper amount of funds. That was how the "My Way To Dreams" DVD was born, as well, as the idea of transferring the whole profit from the book you are holding in your hands, as well as the profit from Lee Andrew's album and his records to the project. When I'm writing these words, our center is sill in the sphere of plans. Though, we are slowly beginning to realize it. Living with Lee in my Warsaw flat, working as a photographer and a Master of a Secular Funeral Ceremony, laughing at the joked placed on the JoeMonster, where I was called a "Loosy Chaplain," I still trust that the faith in people and their will of living in freedom hasn't died inside me. Even, when the Law and Justice unleashed a bomb scandal anew last year, and the Police are following my internet connections, I'm not afraid. I know that together with You, I will manage to reach my goal. The girls from the Lesbijka.org wrote some time ago: "Because my vice is my tendency to fight for everything that we care for." That slogan became my life motto and my indicator for future life.

Epilogue

This book would have never been written, if not a series of events and coincidences, which forced me to write it. Also, it would have never arisen, without the people, who supported me in difficult moments, devoting their time do and help me to go up go further. So, I wouldn't have been able to put the last dot not having said thank you to all of them. If I wanted to list all the names of people and organizations, that I'm grateful to, I would have to write another few tens of pages. That's why, I will restrict myself to a general thank you to all the people, who were standing by me, supporting me and have never let me down. And I especially thank my enemies for teaching me the truth about the world.

I cordially apologize to all the persons, whom I might offend or disgust. As I mentioned at the very beginning, this is a story seen with my eyes. I described it that way I have remembered it. If you don't agree with my story well, the paper is patient and capacious. You can always write your own version of Szymon Niemiec's story.

www.ingramcontent.com/pod-product-compliance
Lightning Source LLC
Chambersburg PA
CBHW051822090426
42736CB00011B/1600